THE ISLANDS OF CROATIA

30 WALKS ON 14 ADRIATIC ISLANDS

About the Author

Rudolf Abraham (www.rudolfabraham.co.uk) is an award-winning travel writer and photographer specialising in Croatia and Eastern Europe. He is the author of eight books (five of them on Croatia) and has contributed to over a dozen more, and his work is published widely in magazines. He first visited Croatia in 1998, lived in Zagreb for two years, and continues to spend several weeks a year in his favourite country in Europe.

Other Cicerone guides by the author

St Oswald's Way and St Cuthbert's Way:
   Long-distance trails in Northumberland and the Borders
The Mountains of Montenegro
Torres del Paine: Trekking in Chile's Premier National Park
Walking in Croatia

THE ISLANDS OF CROATIA

30 WALKS ON 14 ADRIATIC ISLANDS

by Rudolf Abraham

2 POLICE SQUARE, MILNTHORPE, CUMBRIA LA7 7PY
www.cicerone.co.uk

© Rudolf Abraham 2014
First edition 2014
ISBN: 978 1 85284 703 6

Printed by KHL Printing, Singapore
A catalogue record for this book is available from the British Library.
All photographs © Rudolf Abraham

Dedication

For Tamara and Ivana

Route maps for Walks 1–4 from Baška Marked Tourist Footpaths
© Turistička zajednica Općine Baška

Route maps for Walks 5–7 from Otok Rab – Biking and Trekking
© Turistička zajednica grada Raba/Zlatko Smerke (SMAND)

Route maps for Walks 8–9 from 21a Otok Cres (2011)
© Zlatko Smerke (SMAND)

Route maps for Walks 10–12 from Lošinj – Tourist and Trekking Map (2014);
Walk 19 from Brač Bike – Bike Tourist Map (2013);
Walks 20–21 from Hvar Tourist and Trekking Map (2012);
Walks 22–24 from Otok Vis Tourist and Trekking Map (2010);
Walks 25–27 from Korčula Tourist and Trekking Map (2012);
Walk 28 from Park prirode Lastovsko otočje – Tourist and Trekking Map (2010)

all © Rudolf Schwabe (HGSS, Hrvatska Gorska služba spašavanja)

Route maps for Walks 13–14 from Otok Maun 4415-1-2-2 and Pag 4415-2-1-1;
Walk 16 from Veli Iž 4415-2-3-3
© Državna geodetska uprava

Route map for Walk 15 from Island Ugljan Map
© Turistička zajednica Općine Preko

Route maps for Walks 17–18 from Javna ustanova park prirode Telašćica
© Public Institution Nature Park Telašćica

Route maps for Walks 29–30
© Nacionalni park Mljet

Front cover: Looking south to Križići and beyond from the trail to Sis, on the island of Cres (Walk 8)

CONTENTS

Acknowledgements

I would like to thank Rudolf Schwabe, Head of Cartography at the HGSS (Croatian Mountain Rescue Service); Zlatko Smerke at SMAND; Majda Šale, Director of the Baška Tourist Office; Luka Perčinić, Marketing Manager at the Rab Tourist Board; Zrinka Badurina, Director of the Lošinj Tourist Board; Nina Stohera and Ina Sikirić at the Zadar County Tourist Office; Hana Turudić at the Korčula Tourist Office; Dorjan Dragojević at the Vela Luka Tourist Office; Maja Šeparović at the Blato Tourist Office; Tanja Augustinović at the Kvarner County Tourist Office; Bernard Maržić at the Pag Tourist Office; Ante Brižić at the Preko Tourist Office; Ivana Čarić and Lidija at the Sali Tourist Office; Aleksandar Bonačić in Sali; Danijela Vlahović Director of the Stari Grad Tourist Office; Ivan Cvitanić at the Supetar Tourist Office; Ivo Fiamengo at the Vis Tourist Office; Iva Frian at the Lastovo Tourist Office; Dunja at the Cres Tourist Office; Vesna Petešić at the Public Institution Nature Park Telašćica; Andrea Anelić at the Mljet Tourist Board; Mirjana Marković in Zadar; the Barbić family at Camp Skriveni on Lastovo; Nina and Robi Malatestinić in Beli; Igor Vilus at the Croatian State Geodetic Administration; Meri Matešić, Director of the Croatian National Tourist Board; Karmen Carev Smith at the Croatian National Tourist Office in London; and last but not least, my wife and daughter, who ferry-hopped their way around the islands of the Croatian Adriatic with me in the summer of 2013.

Advice to Readers

While every effort is made by our authors to ensure the accuracy of guide-
books as they go to print, changes can occur during the lifetime of an edition. If we know of any, there will be an Updates tab on this book's page
on the Cicerone website (www.cicerone.co.uk), so please check before
planning your trip. We also advise that you check information about such
things as transport, accommodation and shops locally. Even rights of way
can be altered over time. We are always grateful for information about
any discrepancies between a guidebook and the facts on the ground, sent
by email to info@cicerone.co.uk or by post to Cicerone, 2 Police Square,
Milnthorpe LA7 7PY, United Kingdom.

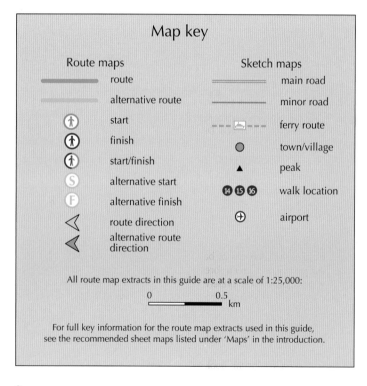

Map key

Route maps	Sketch maps
▬▬▬▬▬ route	══════ main road
▬▬▬▬▬ alternative route	────── minor road
(↑) start	– – 🚢 – – ferry route
(↑) finish	● town/village
(↑) start/finish	▲ peak
(S) alternative start	⑭ ⑮ ⑯ walk location
(F) alternative finish	
◁ route direction	⊕ airport
◁ alternative route direction	

All route map extracts in this guide are at a scale of 1:25,000:

0   0.5
▬▬▬▬▬ km

For full key information for the route map extracts used in this guide,
see the recommended sheet maps listed under 'Maps' in the introduction.

PREFACE

Looking down across the islands of Rava and Iž, and towards Zadar on the mainland, from Dugi otok (Walk 16)

I first visited the islands of the Croatian Adriatic back in the late 1990s, having already fallen in love with Croatia (and a Croatian) and moved to Zagreb. Despite countless return visits over the ensuing years, the sense of excitement at first seeing these scattered whalebacks of bare grey-bronze rock and green forest, dotted with exquisitely well-preserved old towns and etched against some of the most brilliant blue seas imaginable, has never really left me.

Although I have made regular trips to Croatia's islands over a period of some 15 years, writing this book in the summer of 2013 was something of a revelation – there was simply so much here that was both rewarding and inspiring. As you walk across these islands, whether following ancient stonewalled paths between olive groves or boulder-hopping along bare limestone ridges with unforgettable views across the Adriatic – the air alive with butterflies, and each step redolent with the scent of sage, lavender and thyme – I hope you enjoy using this guide as much as I have enjoyed writing it.

Rudolf Abraham
2014

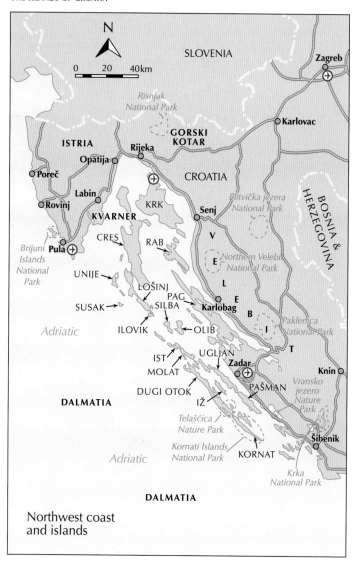

Northwest coast
and islands

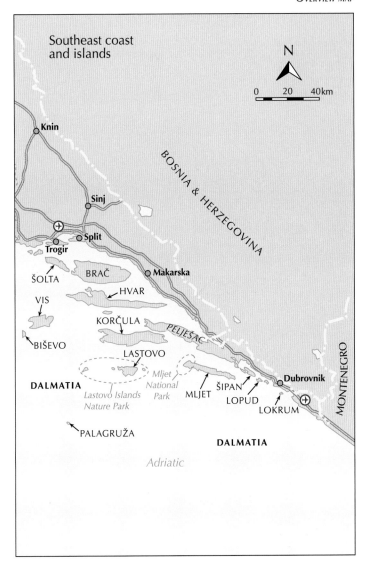

Southeast coast
and islands

N

0   20   40km

Knin

BOSNIA & HERZEGOVINA

Sinj

Split

Trogir

ŠOLTA

BRAČ

Makarska

VIS

HVAR

KORČULA

PELJEŠAC

BIŠEVO

LASTOVO

DALMATIA

Lastovo Islands
Nature Park

Mljet
National
Park

MLJET

ŠIPAN

LOPUD

Dubrovnik

LOKRUM

MONTENEGRO

PALAGRUŽA

DALMATIA

Adriatic

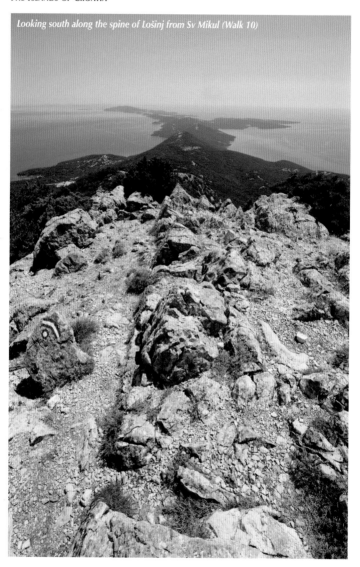

Looking south along the spine of Lošinj from Sv Mikul (Walk 10)

INTRODUCTION

A view of the Kabal peninsula – which stretches north from Stari Grad on the island of Hvar – from Brač (Walk 19)

Croatia's myriad islands form an outstandingly beautiful landscape, stretching along the coast in a fragmented arc from the Kvarner Gulf in the northwest to the walls of Dubrovnik in the southeast. Bare limestone ridges, toothy knolls and rock-strewn plateaus alternate with olive groves, vineyards and areas of lush green forest; sundrenched beaches and rocky coves are punctuated by spectacular sea cliffs; and remote, uninhabited islets protrude, just barely, from some of the most crystal-clear waters anywhere on the Adriatic.

Along with the rest of the country, the islands are incredibly rich in history, having witnessed the rise and fall of cultures, kingdoms and empires across well over two and a half millennia – from Bronze and Iron Age hill tribes and Greek colonists to imperial Rome and mercantile Venice, Croatia's medieval kings and the Dual Monarchy of Austria–Hungary. There is a wealth of architecture to be seen here – medieval walled cities, Roman ruins, Venetian palaces, Romanesque churches and opulent Austrian villas – and colourful festivals are spread throughout the year, several of them inscribed on the UNESCO List of Intangible Cultural Heritage, preserving local tradition and culture. Croatia's islands are also home to a staggering array of wildlife and plants – from birds of prey to butterflies to bottlenose dolphins, including numerous species that are rare or endemic.

The islands are covered by a network of superb hiking trails. Paths are almost uniformly clear and well marked, and the views are frequently spectacular. Yet remarkably, despite many of the paths being almost no distance from busy tourist hot-spots, most see hardly any walkers at all.

CROATIA: KEY FACTS AND FIGURES	
Country name	Republika Hrvatska
Capital	Zagreb
Language	Croatian
Currency	kuna (kn or HNK)
Population	4.29 million (2011 census)
Land surface area	56,594 km²
Length of coastline (including islands)	5835km
Number of islands, islets and reefs	1185
Time zone	GMT +1 (CET)
International telephone code	+385
Electricity	220V/50Hz
Main religion	Roman Catholic (87.8%)

The walks in this guide cover 14 islands spread fairly evenly along the length of the Croatian coast, visiting better-known places such as Hvar, Brač and Mljet, as well as less well-known spots such as Dugi otok and Lastovo. The walks can all be completed within a day, and are almost all easy, with no technical difficulties or scrambling. They range from short, easy coastal strolls with minimal elevation gain to more challenging full-day outings over rocky ridges and summits. The majority of the walks are on footpaths, rather than on unsealed roads and 4WD tracks, and most have access to shops and other facilities (and generally, public transport) at one or the other end of the route.

THE ISLANDS

Croatia's Adriatic coast and islands are the most popular part of the country with visitors, both foreign and domestic. Neveretheless, population density on the islands is low, particularly outside the main holiday season when they return to their sleepy Mediterranean selves. And while there are several extremely popular spots on the coast of the islands, which attract a huge number of visitors during the summer, inland the islands remain largely rural and remarkably little visited.

Even the most popular towns on the coasts of the islands are quite small, and almost universally have outstandingly well-preserved historic cores, often with narrow cobbled streets and lovely Romanesque, Venetian and Hapsburg architecture clustered around a sheltered harbour.

Landscapes and terrain vary considerably between islands, from olive groves and scattered forest to saltwater lakes, rocky ridges and plateaus crisscrossed by ancient drystone walls.

Given the islands' popularity there is no shortage of accommodation, and there are supermarkets, banks and other facilities in the main towns. There are regular ferry services to all 14 islands in the guide, and there are bus services to all but three of the walks described.

The islands follow the same regional divisions as the Adriatic coast, and the walks in the guide are arranged from north to south – starting with those in the region of Kvarner in the north (including Krk, Rab, Cres and Lošinj, Walks 1–12), then covering Northern Dalmatia (including Pag, Ugljan and Dugi otok, Walks 13–18), Central Dalmatia (including Brač, Hvar and Vis, Walks 19–24) and Southern Dalmatia (including Korčula, Lastovo and Mljet, Walks 25–30).

GEOGRAPHY

There are some 1185 islands, islets, isles and reefs on the Croatian Adriatic – the precise figure varying somewhat depending on whether some of the smaller islets and reefs, submerged at low tide (it's easy to forget that the Mediterranean has a tide – albeit a very minimal one in the Adriatic), are included or not. Of these islands 67 are inhabited,

Evening light on the rocky island of Prvić, just off the southern tip of the island of Krk, near Baška

the two largest being Krk and Cres, each with an area of around 405km², followed by Brač (395km²), Hvar (297km²) and Pag (284km²), while at the other end of the scale many of the smaller islands such as Susak, Lopud and Koločep have surface areas of less than 5km².

Generally elongated, the islands follow the northwest–southeast orientation of the coast, and represent all that remains above sea level of a low, outlying range of hills which once formed part of the coastal ranges such as Velebit, Mosor and Biokovo, collectively known as the Dinaric Alps. Terrain (and vegetation – see 'Plants'; page 27) on the islands varies considerably, from relatively flat and low to knobbly hills and crags, long sinewy ridges and spectacular sea cliffs, together with an endless succession of secluded coves, many of them accessible only by boat.

The hills on these islands are not particularly high – the greatest elevation on any of the islands is Vidova gora (780m), on the island of Brač; other prominent 'island highs' include Sv Nikola (628m, on Hvar), Osorščica (589m, on Lošinj), Hum (587m, on Vis) and Obzova (568m, on Krk). While these figures may not seem very high, bear in mind that in most cases climbing them involves starting from just above sea level. In contrast, some of the islands are much lower – the highest point on Unije is only 95m above sea level.

The Croatian coastline is spectacularly indented, with a total length of some 1777km over a distance of only around 526km (the latter figure measured as a straight line from the

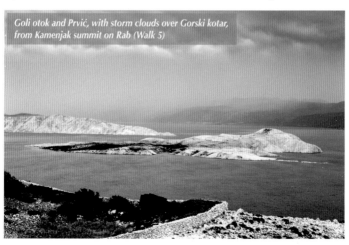

Goli otok and Prvić, with storm clouds over Gorski kotar, from Kamenjak summit on Rab (Walk 5)

Slovenian to the Montenegrin border). This figure rises to 5835km when all the islands are included – the coastlines of the islands alone accounting for over 4000km of this figure. The coastline is rocky, with beaches made up of either rocks or, less frequently, pebbles. Fine shingle or true sandy beaches are rare, some of the best known – and consequently the most popular – being Zlatni rat (at Bol, on the island of Brač), Vela plaža (at Baška, on the island of Krk), Rajska plaža or 'Paradise beach' (at Lopar, on the island of Rab), Sv Duh (near Novalja, on Pag) and Saharun (on Dugi otok).

The islands are formed mainly of Cretaceous limestone – laid down on the seabed in the form of shells and other marine life when the Adriatic, along with the rest of this part of Central and Eastern Europe, was submerged beneath a shallow tropical sea some 66–145 million years ago. The Croatian Adriatic had become a coastal plain by the Pleistocene Era (2.5 million–11,700 years ago), with the gradual flooding of this coastal plain during the Holocene leading around 7000 years ago to the creation of the islands and the Adriatic Sea as we now know it.

Croatia is karst country. Karst is formed by the gradual dissolving of the limestone rock by rainwater – or, more specifically, by the combination of rainwater and carbon dioxide from the earth's atmosphere and the soil, which results in a weak solution of carbonic acid. Over millennia this process gradually enlarges surface drainage holes, as well as horizontal and vertical cracks and fissures in the rock, as the water percolates downwards, creating distinctive surface features such as vertical fluting (karren), solution pans, limestone pavement and sinkholes (doline), while beneath the surface it leads to the formation of an extensive network of caves and underground drainage channels, with all rainwater rapidly disappearing underground.

Collapses in the roof of these subterranean voids leads to the formation of larger sinkholes and cenotes. (Most of the deeper caves and sinkholes in Croatia are on the mainland, and some of these are extremely deep – Lukina jama on Velebit is among the 15 deepest sinkholes in the world.) *Polje* – large, level-floored depressions up to several kilometres in size, where a thin layer of alluvial soil has gradually accumulated – often form the only suitable areas for growing vegetables and the cultivation of crops.

Many of these features will be encountered while walking on the islands – for example Jama Komoračišće, a prominent sinkhole on Kom, Korčula (Walk 27), and limestone pavement on Šćah, Ugljan (Walk 15), to name but two. On the island of Rab a number of such karst and other geological features are highlighted on marked geological trails (Walk 7).

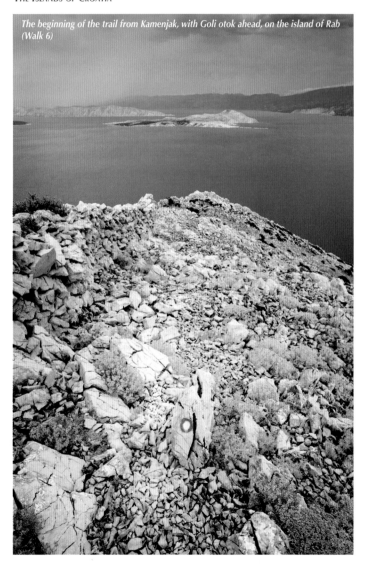

The beginning of the trail from Kamenjak, with Goli otok ahead, on the island of Rab (Walk 6)

The island of Susak (and part of Unije) is unusual in being composed largely of sand and loess laid over a limestone base; while the quarries of Brač have long been famed for their white marble, much prized by sculptors and used to build Diocletian's palace in Split during antiquity and, more recently, part of the White House in Washington DC.

CLIMATE

The Croatian coast and islands experience a Mediterranean climate, and this is distinct and separate from the inland continental climate, which is significantly colder during the winter. The islands are protected from this colder climate by the mountain barrier of the coastal ranges (the Dinaric Alps).

Summers on the coast and islands are hot and dry, with average mean temperatures of between 21°C and 22°C on the northern and central Dalmatian islands in June and September, and average mean temperatures of between 24°C and 25°C for the same area in July and August. At least half the days in July and August reach 30°C or above, although the highest temperatures recorded are not above 37°C–38°C. Even outside the summer months it is a balmy 18°C and 17°C in October and May respectively, and 14°C in April. Expect temperatures to be slightly higher in the south (Korčula, Dubrovnik) and very slightly cooler further north (Cres, Rijeka) – although these differences may be minimal. Hvar is supposed to have the most hours of sunshine on the Croatian Adriatic – around

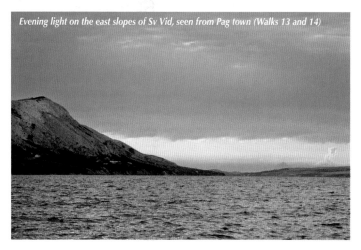

Evening light on the east slopes of Sv Vid, seen from Pag town (Walks 13 and 14)

2715 per year – with most other islands in central Dalmatia not far behind. Sea-water temperatures in central Dalmatia are usually around 22°C in June and September, and up above 24°C in July and August – most Croats would consider sea-water temperatures of anything less than 20°C decidedly chilly.

Whereas the heat can frequently become intense in early August on the mainland coast and in cities such as Split and Dubrovnik, summer temperatures on the islands are generally moderated by a light breeze, making them significantly more pleasant. These general observations do not hold true on islands with less vegetation, such as Pag or Goli otok ('naked island'), where the heat during the summer months can be well and truly fierce.

Winters on the coast and islands are relatively mild, although frequently rainy (with less rain on the islands than the coast). January is the coldest month, with an average mean temperature of around 8.5°C on northern and central Dalmatian islands. November tends to be the wettest month. Snow is rare in the mainland coastal area (not so the mountains just inland from the coast, which see significant snowfall during the winter months) and rarer still on the islands – even Split and Dubrovnik are unlikely to see more than one day of snow, on average, in January.

Several winds can buffet the Croatian coast and islands at any time of year, the strongest (and most disruptive) of which is the *bura* – a cold northeasterly, which descends upon the Adriatic from the cols and high passes of Velebit in gusts which frequently reach gale force. The Venetian traveller Alberto Abbé Fortis, writing in the 18th century, even claimed that on occasions the bura would pick up young children and dash them against the walls of houses, and throw down horses loaded with salt. There is a saying in Croatia that the bura is born in Lika (the region behind the Velebit mountains), lives on Velebit and dies on the sea – but you can expect it to give the eastern coasts of Krk, Rab, Pag and some other islands a pretty good battering, too. When the bura really does blow, expect choppy (and cooler) seas, possible disruption to ferry and catamaran services, and possible closures of bridges to traffic (including buses) on the main coastal highway.

Other winds include the *jugo*, a moderate southerly (*jug* meaning 'south') that typically brings cloud and rain to the coastal mountains and is traditionally associated with bad temper and ill health. (In the Republic of Dubrovnik during the Middle Ages, crimes committed when the jugo was blowing generally earned a more lenient sentence for their perpetrator, following the belief that the wind had, at least partially, driven them to commit the crime or induced their fit of rage.) The *maestral* is a brisk sea breeze that tends to

Trees bent by the bura wind, on the rocky northeast coast of Rab (Walk 6)

blow from the morning to the early afternoon; the *široko* is a warm, dry southeasterly from north Africa, roughly equivalent to the sirocco in other parts of the Mediterranean.

WHEN TO VISIT

On balance, the best time to visit Croatia's islands is between April and October, with May, June and September being the best for walking, and July/August being the hottest and busiest (most Croatians take their holidays on the Croatian coast in early August). Wildflowers will be at their most impressive in June. Many hotels and private rooms close during the winter, although prices will be lower than in high season at those which do remain open, and competition for rooms much less. Some ferries

operate a reduced service outside the summer months. On public holidays (see 'Croatian national holidays'; page 50) expect shops to be closed and public transport to be considerably restricted.

WILDLIFE

Croatia has an incredibly rich biodiversity for a country its size, with over 38,000 known species of plants and animals, including around 1000 which are endemic, and many species that are threatened or endangered. The Croatian islands are particularly interesting for the profusion of reptiles and invertebrates that can be seen, and for their extraordinarily rich plant life, while the surrounding waters of the Adriatic are inhabited by a wealth of marine life.

21

Mammals

Mammals including Red and Roe deer, Wild pig and Fox can be found on various islands on the Croatian Adriatic, along with smaller species such as Red squirrel, Pine marten and Common dormouse. There are several species of bat (at least five species on Lastovo alone), including Greater and Mediterranean horseshoe bat, Savi's pipistrelle and Long-fingered bat (the latter classified as vulnerable on the International Union for Conservation of Nature (IUCN) Red List). Mouflon (wild sheep, ancestor of modern domestic breeds) can be seen on Dugi otok and Lastovo, having been introduced for hunting in the 19th century, and a few of the islands are home to an elusive and little-known carnivore, the European jackal (*Canis aureus*, also known as the Golden jackal). None of the other large carnivores present in small numbers on the Croatian mainland – Brown bear, Grey wolf and Lynx – are found on the islands. The island of Mljet is conspicuous as the only place in Europe where the Indian grey mongoose is found in the wild, having been introduced in the early 20th century to exterminate the island's burgeoning native population of snakes. Incidentally, Croatia's currency (the kuna) is named after the Pine marten – *kuna* in Croatian – the pelts of which were used as a unit of trade and measure of currency in the Middle Ages.

Domesticated livestock includes large numbers of sheep and, in declining numbers since they are now little used to work the land, donkeys (the best place to see the latter is around Mir jezero on Dugi otok).

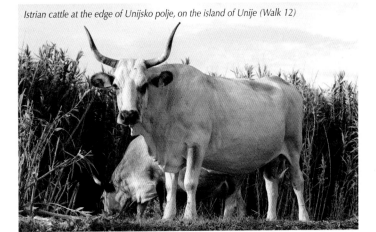

Istrian cattle at the edge of Unijsko polje, on the island of Unije (Walk 12)

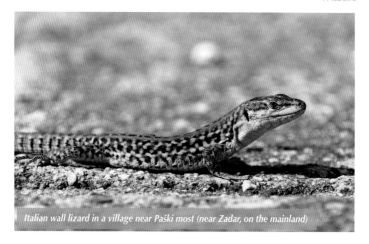

Italian wall lizard in a village near Paški most (near Zadar, on the mainland)

Reptiles and amphibians

Croatia's rocky limestone landscape provides a superb habitat for reptiles, of which Croatia has 41 species (nine of them endemic), with the greatest concentration of these being on the Dalmatian coast and islands.

Croatia has an impressive number of snakes, most of them harmless. Venomous snakes are absent entirely from some of the islands (Lastovo, Mljet, Vis), and on those islands where they are found they are less common than on the mainland. Non-poisonous species include the Four-lined snake, one of the largest European snakes, although completely harmless and easily recognisable by the yellowish-brown stripes along its back; the Leopard snake, which has distinctive brownish-red, dark-edged markings; and Balkan, Western and Large whip snake.

Two venomous species of snake are found on the islands in Croatia: the Nose-horned viper (*Vipera ammodytes*, known locally as *poskok*), which is highly venomous and has been recorded on several islands including Pag, Krk, Brač, Hvar and Korčula; and the Common viper or Adder (*Vipera berus*). The Nose-horned viper is either light grey or brownish copper, with a dark-black zigzag pattern along its back, and is easily recognisable by the soft horn at the end of its snout. It is found on rocky hillsides, under low bushes and around drystone walls. The Montpellier snake, while also venomous (although much less so), has fangs at the back of its jaws rather than the front, so it is extremely unlikely for a human to be bitten unless the snake is actually picked up. Walking boots and hiking poles will usually alert a

Hermann's tortoise in the village of Jovići, near Paški most (Pag bridge)

snake of your approach and give it time to slither off, and snakes will usually only bite in self-defence.

A number of lizards are common (several of them endemic), among them the Balkan green lizard (easily recognisable by its sheer size, up to 16cm or more in length, as much as by its striking green colour) and only slightly smaller Green lizard. Smaller, more commonly seen species include the Common, Italian and Dalmatian wall lizard – the latter two species are quite hard to tell apart, both having black and green stripes along their bodies – and the darker-coloured Sharp-snouted rock lizard. The Lastovo wall lizard is endemic to the island of Lastovo. Other species of reptile include Turkish gecko, European glass lizard and Hermann's tortoise.

Amphibians inhabiting the islands are less commonly seen, but include the European green toad (recognisable by its distinctive marbled pattern), Agile frog (pale brown, with a slightly pointed snout), the smaller (less than 5cm) European tree frog and a subspecies of the common newt.

A useful resource for identifying the reptiles and amphibians of Europe is www.herp.it.

Birds

The cliffs at Beli on the island of Cres constitute the last remaining habitat of the enormous Griffon vulture (*Gyps fulvus*) in Croatia. The birds are huge, with a wingspan of some 2.5 metres, and feed on carrion (historically, sheep carcasses, although a decline in sheep farming has meant there are fewer of these today). If approaching the cliffs by boat it is essential that engines are switched off and that the boat doesn't get too close, otherwise it's not uncommon for the young birds to try to escape their nests before they're able to fly – and fall into the sea and drown. Smaller birds of prey include Common buzzard, Sparrowhawk, Peregrine falcon and Eleonora's falcon.

Waders and wildfowl can be found in areas of brackish marshland such as Saline on Veliki Brijuni and Veliko blato among the saltpans of Pag, including Little egret, Grey heron, Purple heron and Great crested grebe, as well as rarer species such as Great white egret. Seabirds and shorebirds include Black-headed and Yellow-legged gull, Eurasian black tern, Cory's shearwater and Pygmy cormorant, as well as the rare Audouin's gull on the islets of the Lastovo archipelago.

Other species of bird include the Eagle owl (Europe's largest species of owl, recognisable by its size and its prominent ear tufts), Eurasian hoopoe (recognisable by its distinctive black-and-white striped wings and prominent crest), European bee-eater (which has particularly bright-coloured plumage), Alpine swift (an extremely fast-flying bird, distinguishable from the Common swift by the white patch on its breast), Rock thrush and Rock partridge (the latter listed as near-threatened on the IUCN Red List).

For more information on birdlife in Croatia see www.croatiabirding. com.

Invertebrates

Croatia has a vast number of invertebrates – over 15,000 land-dwelling invertebrates have been recorded, plus another 1800 or so freshwater

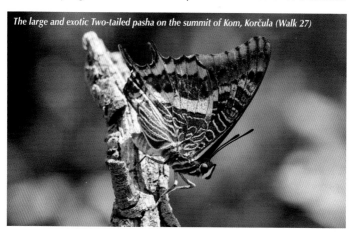

The large and exotic Two-tailed pasha on the summit of Kom, Korčula (Walk 27)

Winter damselfly on Dragodid, the headland north of Komiža, on the island of Vis (Walk 24)

invertebrates and over 5600 seawater invertebrates. Over 600 of them are endemic, with underground karst habitats being particularly rich in endemic species. Invertebrates are also the least studied group of Croatian animals, and several new species have been discovered in recent years – which suggests that there are many species which are as yet undiscovered.

Croatia has over 180 species of butterfly (compared to 56 in the UK), and many of them can be seen on the islands – including such exotic, localised species as the Scarce swallowtail (easily recognisable by the distinctive, very long protruding 'tail' at the back of each wing), Southern swallowtail (with shorter 'tails'), Two-tailed pasha (a large, fast-flying dark butterfly with orange wingtips and two prongs or tails at the back of its wings, which can be spotted on some island hilltops) and endemic Dalmatian ringlet. Croatia also has 71 species of dragonfly and damselfly (compared to 38 species of dragonfly in the UK), and those on the islands include Small spreadwing, Small red damsel, Winter damselfly and several classified as endangered on the IUCN Red List, such as Bladetail and Black pennant.

The European garden spider (also known as Cross-web spider) is common, its web (as the name implies) frequently slung between trees and branches across hiking trails, although it is completely harmless (and, thankfully, larger individuals tend to have their webs above head height). The European black widow spider (*Latrodectus tredecimguttatus*), the bite of which can be extremely dangerous, is also found in Dalmatia, albeit highly localised and in very small numbers (for example, in some areas around Zadar). There are also numerous species of ant – some 35 species on the Kornati islands alone.

For more information on butterflies, including photos for identifying different species, see www.eurobutterflies.com (and the Lepidapp app www.lepidapp.co.uk), www.lepidoptera.pl and www.leps.it.

Fish and other marine life

The waters of the Croatian Adriatic are abundant in fish and other marine life, including several species found only in the eastern Adriatic. Nevertheless, overfishing has resulted in several of these species becoming quite rare or even threatened – including some, such as John Dory and monkfish, that appear on menus at most seafood restaurants. (The Marine Conservation Society publishes a handy booklet on which fish you might want to consider avoiding eating, which can be downloaded for free at www.fishonline. org/pocket-goodfishguide.)

Bottlenose dolphins are a not uncommon sight on the Croatian Adriatic, which is also home to the critically endangered Green turtle, as well as the Loggerhead turtle, and there have been sightings of the critically endangered Mediterranean monk seal in Croatian waters.

The Blue World Institute of Marine Research and Conservation (www.blue-world.org) runs several scientific, educational and conservation projects from the islands of Lošinj and Vis, including the Adriatic Dolphin Project. The Marine Education Centre at Veli Lošinj (opened in 2003) was the first marine education centre on the eastern Adriatic coast, and the Cres-Lošinj Marine Protected Area was the first such area for dolphins in the entire Mediterranean. They also run an 'adopt a dolphin' programme.

PLANTS

Croatia has over 8800 recorded plant species and some 4500 recorded species of fungi (the actual number in

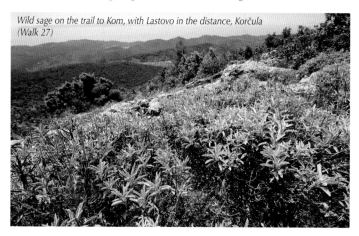

Wild sage on the trail to Kom, with Lastovo in the distance, Korčula (Walk 27)

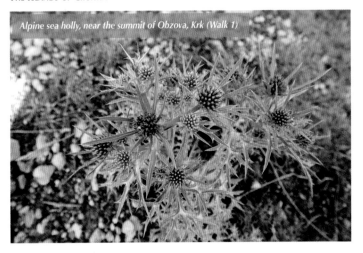
Alpine sea holly, near the summit of Obzova, Krk (Walk 1)

both cases is likely to be significantly higher), making it one of the richest areas of plant life in Europe in terms of species in relation to land area. The number of species on the Adriatic islands is particularly high (for example, there are 810 species of plant on the small island of Lastovo alone, between 700 and 800 on the Kornati islands, and around 1300 on the island of Cres), and the islands also have one of the highest proportions of endemic species in the country.

Much of the vegetation on the islands consists of maquis – dense hardy shrubs and bushes, including the Strawberry tree (easily recognisable by its distinctive red, strawberry-like berries), Myrtle, and Prickly and Phoenecian juniper – and low evergreen trees, most characteristically Holm oak (also known as Holly oak)

and Downy oak, interspersed with Oriental hornbeam, Manna ash and stands of Aleppo pine. Wild herbs such as rosemary, lavender, bay, sage and thyme grow in profusion, along with fennel and wild asparagus, augmented by olive trees (there are several different varieties), carob and fig.

Some of the islands have more extensive areas of forest – the most heavily forested islands on the Croatian Adriatic are Mljet, the western half of Rab, and Korčula. At the opposite extreme are islands such as the appropriately named Goli otok (meaning 'naked island') and Pag, where vegetation is extremely sparse. Rab is a good illustration of these extreme contrasts – the lower western half of the island, and in particular the Kalifron peninsula, is incredibly lush and green, while the higher eastern side of the island, and in particular the steep slopes above the east coast, is rocky and largely bare. The little that does grow there is bent double by the harsh northeast wind, the bura.

Plants on the islands include Alpine sea holly, Dubrovnik knapweed (also known as Star thistle, endemic to Croatia), Illyrian cotton-thistle, Immortelle, Spanish broom, Spiny spurge, the so-called 'Curry plant', several species of bellflower and numerous species of orchid.

NATIONAL PARKS AND NATURE PARKS

Croatia has eight national parks (*nacionalni park*, usually abbreviated to the prefix NP) and 11 nature parks (*park prirode*, or PP). The islands are home to five of these:

- Kornati Islands National Park (NP Kornati, www.kornati.hr)
- Mljet National Park (NP Mljet, www.np-mljet.hr)
- Brijuni Islands National Park (NP Brijuni, www.brijuni.hr)
- Telašćica Nature Park (PP Telašćica, www.telascica.hr)
- Lastovo Islands Nature Park (PP Lastovsko otočje, www.pp-lastovo.hr)

There are also many reserves and specially protected areas, including Dundo Forest Reserve (Kalifron peninsula, Rab), Koćje (Korčula), Veliko blato (Pag), Kuntrep Ornithological Reserve (Krk), and the Kruna and Podokladi Ornithological Reserves (Cres).

An entry fee is payable on entering a national park (and some nature parks), and you should hang on to your ticket as you may be asked to

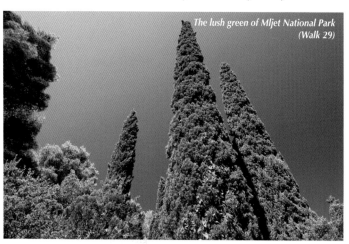

The lush green of Mljet National Park (Walk 29)

29

show it later. Camping is prohibited in national parks and nature parks.

While the wildlife and geological features of a natural/nature park are undoubtedly of exceptional interest and beauty, this does not necessarily in itself make an island the best destination for hiking. In fact, some of the best hikes are on islands that are not designated national/nature parks.

Many of Croatia's other national/nature parks are on, or easily accessible from, the mainland coast, and you can easily combine your stay on the islands with a visit to one or more of these: Krka, Paklenica, Plitvička jezera, Risnjak and Sjeverni Velebit national parks, and Biokovo, Učka and Vransko jezero nature parks.

Evidence of the presence of Neolithic man is widespread on the islands of the Croatian Adriatic, where they hunted for game, fished in its waters, and sheltered in its many limestone caves.

Settlements grew during the Bronze Age and Iron Age, and from around 800BC the history of the eastern Adriatic becomes synonymous with the Illyrians, an Indo-European people, composed of numerous tribes scattered throughout the region from the Veneto to Albania. Among the most important of these tribes were the Liburni (famed pirates, who originally controlled the coast and islands

The Croatian Apoxyomenos – an intact life-sized bronze Roman statue, discovered in waters near Lošinj

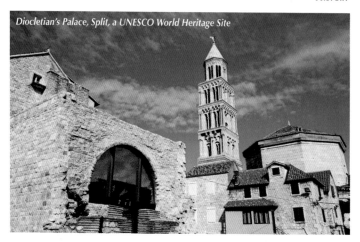
Diocletian's Palace, Split, a UNESCO World Heritage Site

from Istria to the River Krka), as well as the Delmatae, the Japodes and the Ardiaei. Traces of many of their hill forts still remain on the Adriatic islands, and a number of them have left their names in the region ('Dalmatia' from Delmatae; 'Adriatic' from Ardiaei).

Greek settlers arrived in the fourth century BC, establishing colonies on several of the islands including Korkyra meliana (Korčula), Issa (Vis) and Pharos (Hvar), as well as on the coast at Epidaurus (Cavtat), Tragurion (Trogir) and elsewhere.

Rome launched a series of campaigns across the Adriatic against the Illyrians, beginning in 229BC and leading to the establishment of the Roman province of Illyricum, with its capital at Salona on the edge of modern Split. The remains of Roman villas, palaces and other buildings are widespread on the coast and islands, including the incredibly well-preserved amphitheatre at Pula and the UNESCO-listed Diocletian's Palace in Split.

After the fall of Rome in the fourth century AD the region witnessed a succession of invasions – Visigoths, Huns, Ostrogoths – until Byzantium gained control of the Croatian coast and islands, ushering in an a spell of relative peace and prosperity from the sixth century until the arrival of another horde, the Avars, at the beginning of the seventh century.

The Slavs arrived on the Adriatic some time in the seventh century, having crossed the Danube and gradually settled in the rest of Croatia over the preceding two centuries. Most of the Dalmatian coast and islands were ceded by Byzantium to the Franks in 812, although Byzantium regained its control of Dalmatia around half a century later, when it became one of a number of Byzantine 'themes', with its capital at Zadar.

The second half of the ninth century saw a gradual increase in the power and autonomy of local Croatian dukes, reflected in a move towards religious autonomy and the adoption of Glagolitic (the written form of Old Church Slavonic) instead of Latin by the local priests. In 888 Duke Branimir pledged his loyalty to the Pope and assumed the title Duke of the Croats; Tomislav became the first king of Croatia in 925; and during the reign of Petar Krešimir IV (1058–1074) Dalmatian and Pannonian (inland) Croatia were for the first time unified into a single state, although it is not certain that all the islands were included in this.

Petar was succeeded by Zvonimir (1075–1089), who had the title King of Croatia and Dalmatia conferred upon him by Pope Gregory VII, but his kingdom more or less fell to pieces during the power struggles which followed his death, and in 1091 Hungary invaded Croatia, with the Hungarian Arpad dynasty inheriting the rights of the Croatian kings in 1102.

It was during this period that the city of Dubrovnik (or Ragusa) rose to power. Founded in the first half of the seventh century by refugees from Epidaurus (Cavtat), a city recently devastated by the Avars and the Slavs, Dubrovnik soon grew rich on maritime trade, and in the 12th century developed into an independent republic. In 1190 Dubrovnik signed treaties against external enemies, in particular Venice, and by the 14th century its territory stretched from the Kotor inlet in Montenegro to the northern tip of the Pelješac peninsula, and included the islands of Lastovo and Mljet.

In the 12th century Venice launched a series of attacks on the coastal cities of Dalmatia, as well as on a number of its islands, sacking Zadar in 1202 as part of the infamous Fourth Crusade (which would go on to sack Constantinople two years later) and taking Dubrovnik in 1205. Venice is credited with having sourced much of the wood for its magnificent fleet from the islands of the Croatian Adriatic.

The Mongols arrived on the Adriatic coast during the 13th century, which they ravaged while in hot pursuit of King Bela of Hungary. There was a brief return to Hungarian rule in the 14th century, with Venice temporarily relinquishing its grip on Dalmatia, but by 1420 Venice controlled the whole of Dalmatia – with the exception of Dubrovnik, which became an independent republic with its own government from 1358 – a grip it would not relinquish until the arrival of Napoleon.

The Ottoman conquest of the Balkans during the second half of the 15th century saw the displacement of large numbers of people. Some of them, such as the Glagolitic priests from the Poljica Republic (the

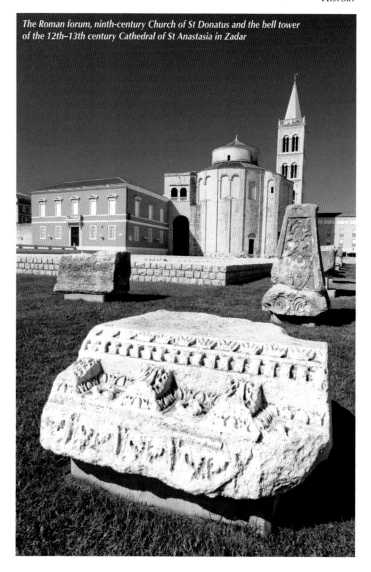

The Roman forum, ninth-century Church of St Donatus and the bell tower of the 12th–13th century Cathedral of St Anastasia in Zadar

Relief sculpture in the town of Vis

mountainous area inland from Split), took refuge on the islands, the latter on Brač, where they founded a monastery at Pustinja Blaca. Others became famed pirates – the Uskoks of Senj, scourge of Ottoman (and Venetian) shipping for years ('God keep you from the hands of Senj', went an old Venetian saying).

Napoleon extinguished the Venetian Republic in 1797, and his victory over Austria in 1805 resulted in Dalmatia being ceded to France, and the creation of the Illyrian Provinces. He dissolved the Republic of Dubrovnik the following year. Napoleon instigated a number of reforms in Dalmatia, including the establishment of schools and the University of Zadar to combat illiteracy; the draining of the marshes to combat rampant malaria; even a tree-plantation programme, in an attempt to restore the denuded forests. Yet these reforms remained largely unpopular, due in part to French opposition to the clergy, and to the fact that new taxes were introduced upon the locals in order to pay for the reforms.

Dalmatia was returned to Austria in 1815 following the Congress of Vienna, with the Istrian coast and the island of Lošinj developing into favourite resorts for the well-heeled Austrian elite, while ship-building boomed in Rijeka and Mali Lošinj. However, the ongoing imposition of Hungarian language and culture in Croatia, and the fact that most upper-class Dalmatians spoke Italian, led to the rise of the Illyrian Movement, with calls for the teaching of Slavic language at schools, and for the unification of Dalmatia with Slavonia (inland Croatia, which was now under Hungarian control again).

With the collapse of the Austro-Hungarian Empire at the end of the First World War in 1918, a Croatian delegation made an agreement with the Serbian government for the establishment of a parliamentary monarchy ruling over the two countries, and in December 1918 the first communal Yugoslav state, the Kingdom of Serbs, Croats and Slovenes, was founded. It was to last until 1941, although it was never recognised by the Treaty of Versailles. However, the Treaty of Rapallo in 1920 gave Istria, Zadar and a number of islands to Italy, and a new constitution abolished the Croatian *sabor* (parliament) and centralised power in Belgrade, leading to opposition to the new regime.

Germany invaded Yugoslavia in April 1941, installing the Ustaše as rulers of the Fascist NDH (Independent State of Croatia), headed by Ante Pavelić, who between 1941 and 1945 implemented a range of decrees against the 'enemies' of the regime (primarily Jews, Gypsies and Serbs), including the establishment of several extermination camps. However, the Ustaše drew their support from only a minority of the population, centred around Lika and western Herzegovina, and owed their authority largely to the support of Hitler and Mussolini. That their support would remain minimal in Dalmatia was guaranteed by an agreement to cede large chunks of the coast and islands to Italy. Armed resistance to the Ustaše was taken up by the Četniks, soon to be superseded by the National Liberation Partisans under Josip Broz Tito, to whom Allied support was channelled and who by 1943 controlled much of Croatia. In 1944 Tito made a cave on the remote island of Vis his clandestine base for operations.

Following the end of the Second World War, the Federal Peoples' Republic of Yugoslavia was established on 29 Nov 1945, consisting

Titova špilja, used as a base by Tito during the Second World War, on the slopes of Hum, Vis (Walk 22)

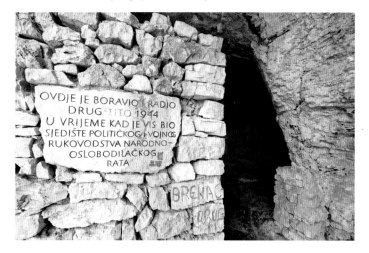

35

of six republics and two autonomous provinces. Tito initiated a number of constitutional reforms and formally broke with Stalinism in 1948. But the perceived over-representation of Serbs in government positions and the security forces, combined with the suppression of organised religion, led to increasing dissatisfaction in Croatia, culminating in the 'Croatian Spring' of 1971. Following Tito's death in 1980, discontent and nationalist aspirations which he had largely driven underground in 1971 slowly rose to the surface.

Free elections were held in April 1990, with Franjo Tuđman and the HDZ (Croatian Democratic Union) elected to office with 40 per cent of the vote. Mass dismissals of Serbs from the public service sector, combined with an unrelenting Serbian media campaign heralding the rebirth of the Ustaše, prompted Croatia's 600,000 strong Serb community in the Krajina and eastern Slavonia to demand autonomy. In May 1991, following the deaths of 12 Croatian policemen near Osijek, a referendum was held, with over 90 per cent voting in favour of Croatian independence, which was formally declared on 25 June 1991. In response, the Krajina Serbs held their own referendum and voted to remain part of Yugoslavia. JNA (Yugoslav People's Army) forces entered Slovenia, which had also declared its independence, but were comprehensively defeated in five days. In Croatia, the so-called

'Homeland War' was to take a very different course.

In June 1991 heavy fighting broke out in the Krajina and eastern Slavonia, after which the Serb-dominated JNA increasingly intervened on its own authority in support of Serbian irregulars. European Community mediation persuaded Croatia to freeze its declaration of independence to prevent the country spiralling into further bloodshed, but in the three months following 25 June a quarter of Croatian territory fell to Serb militias and the JNA. In September, the Croatian government ordered the blockade of federal military installations within Croatia; in response the JNA blockaded the Adriatic and laid siege to the historic town of Vukovar on the Danube. The United Nations declared an arms embargo on all republics of the former Yugoslavia.

In October the JNA and Montenegrin militia positioned themselves on the hills above Dubrovnik, beginning a siege that would last until June the following year and draw widespread international media attention. In November Vukovar finally fell, having been almost razed to the ground by relentless air and artillery bombardment, and many of the surviving inhabitants were massacred. By December, thousands of people had died in the fighting in Croatia, and more than half a million fled their homes.

A ceasefire and UN negotiations in early 1992 were accompanied by

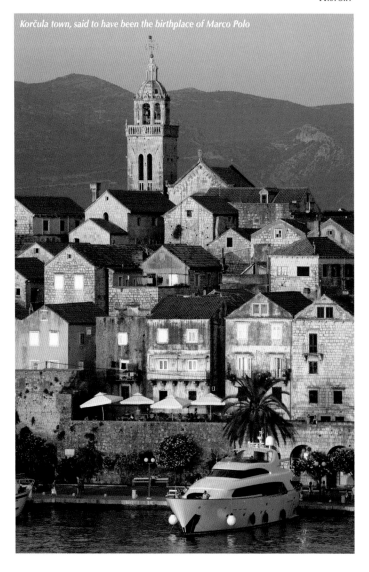

Korčula town, said to have been the birthplace of Marco Polo

the withdrawal of the JNA, although significantly it did not mark a return to pre-war borders or provide for their future settlement. In May 1995 Croatian forces took matters into their own hands and entered occupied western Slavonia, quickly regaining control of the area; the Krajina Serbs responded by shelling Zagreb. In August Croatia retook the Serb stronghold of Knin. In December 1995 the Dayton Accord was signed in Paris, and Croatia's international borders were recognised.

The years since 1995 have seen most of the physical scars of the war repaired, at least on the coast – although many parts of Vukovar in eastern Slavonia still remain in ruins. Tourist numbers and foreign property buying have soared, and local salaries have risen. Croatia achieved candidacy status for EU membership in 2004, finally joining the EU in July 2013.

LANGUAGE

Croatian is a South Slavonic language, closely related to Serbian and Bosnian. The relationship between Croatian and Serbian is variously seen as similar to that between British and American English, or as that between two wholly separate and distinct languages, depending on one's point of view. The standardisation of language while Croatia was part of the Federal Republic of Yugoslavia (1945–1991) resulted in the amalgamation of Croatian and Serbian (as the two dominant languages within the Federation) into Serbo-Croatian or Serbo-Croat. This was written in the Latinised

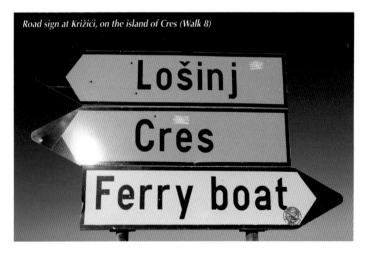

Road sign at Križići, on the island of Cres (Walk 8)

Croatian alphabet in Croatia, and in Cyrillic in Serbia. Since independence, there has been a concerted effort on both sides of the border to untangle, and in some cases polarise, the two languages.

English is widely spoken in Croatia, particularly in Zagreb and major tourist centres on the coast (although less so in smaller towns and villages off the main tourist trail). However, as anywhere making the effort to learn at least a few words of the local language will be appreciated by locals and make travel more rewarding.

Croatian is a phonetic language – that is, every letter in a word is pronounced, and the pronunciation of a given letter is always the same (which makes it far more consistent than English). A number of letters occurring in English are pronounced completely differently in Croatian, most notably 'c' (pronounced 'ts') and 'j' (pronounced 'y'), so learning the correct pronunciation of these will greatly improve your chances of being understood properly.

See Appendix E for a list of useful Croatian words and phrases.

GETTING THERE

By plane

Visitors can fly to Croatia and take a ferry to the islands from the Adriatic coast. There are several major airports on the coast – (north to south)

Pula, Rijeka (the airport for which is actually on the island of Krk), Zadar, Split and Dubrovnik. For the walks in this book, Split, Zadar and Rijeka (see Appendix B for information on these gateway cities) are the most convenient, as they are the main departure points for the islands by ferry (see 'Getting around' for more information on ferries and Appendix C for ferry routes). Visitors who plan to see a bit more of the country than just the coast and islands should consider flying to Croatia's lovely capital, Zagreb, and making their way to the coast from there by bus or train (see 'Getting around' for more details on local transport).

Croatia Airlines (www.croatiaairlines.com) has direct flights from London (and other European cities including Paris, Brussels and Frankfurt) to Zagreb and (either direct, or via Zagreb) all major Croatian cities including Split, Zadar and Rijeka. British Airways (www.ba.com) also flies to Zagreb and Dubrovnik for roughly the same fare as Croatia Airlines. Ryanair (www.ryanair.com) flies from the UK to Zadar, Rijeka and Pula; Easyjet (www.easyjet.com) to Zagreb, Split and Dubrovnik; and Wizz (www.wizzair.com) to Split. Other airlines operating routes from the UK include Flybe (www.flybe.com), Jet2 (www.jet2.com) and Monarch (www.monarch.co.uk), and (via Cologne/Bonn) German Wings (www.germanwings.com). Flights get heavily booked in the summer – so book as far in advance as possible. Note also that schedules (especially those of the low-cost airlines) are subject to frequent change. Always check online.

By train

Visitors can get to Croatia by train from Western Europe. However, note that a train ticket from the UK will almost certainly be more expensive than a flight unless you're willing to be very flexible with travel dates, and you'll need to change trains a few times. The train is likely to be a more attractive option for those arriving from cities in neighbouring countries, such as Trieste, Venice, Ljubljana, Budapest, Belgrade and Sarajevo. See the Rail Europe (www.raileurope.co.uk) and especially the Deutsche Bahn (www.bahn.com) websites for possible routes and fares. Better value

is an InterRail (www.raileurope.co.uk) or a Eurail (www.eurail.com, which must be bought outside Europe) pass, which allows travellers to stop off and explore several other countries on their way to Croatia. InterRail tickets, once the privilege of those under the age of 26, are now available to all age groups.

By bus

International coach services run to Croatia from the UK, Germany and other countries in Western Europe (see www.eurolines.com) – although the fare from London is not much less than a flight.

By ferry

There are several regular ferry crossings between Croatia and Italy – note that some of the following routes only operate in the summer.

Catamarans in front of the harbour building and Diocletian's Palace, Split

The Croatian state ferry company Jadrolinija (www.jadrolinija.hr) sails from Bari to Dubrovnik twice weekly, from where the ferry continues up the coast via Korčula, Stari grad (Hvar) and Split to Rijeka. It also operates services between Ancona, Stari grad (Hvar) and Split, and between Ancona and Zadar. Azzurra Line (www.azzuraline.com) also sails between Bari and Dubrovnik. Emilia Romagna Lines (www.emiliaromagnalines.it) sails from Ravenna, Rimini and Pesaro to Rovinj, Zadar and Rab; SNAV (www.snav.it) sails between Ancona and Split; Blue Line (www.blueline-ferries.com) sails from Ancona to Split, and Ancona to Hvar; Sanmar (www.sanmar.it) sails between Pescara, Hvar and Split. Venezia Lines (www.venezialines.com) sails from Venice to Pula, and from Venice to Poreč and Rovinj; Trieste Lines (www.triestelines.it) sails from Trieste to Rovinj and Pula; Commodore Cruises (www.commodore-cruises.hr) operates ferries between Venice and Pula, Rovinj Poreč and Umag.

GETTING AROUND

By ferry

Travelling by ferry along the Croatian coast and between the mainland and islands is one of the most enjoyable and rewarding ways of exploring the Croatian Adriatic, and in the case of the islands (with the exception of Krk and Pag, which are connected to the mainland by bridge, or unless you happen to have your own boat) it's the only way to get there. All of the major inhabited islands – including all the islands featured in this guide – are accessible from the mainland by

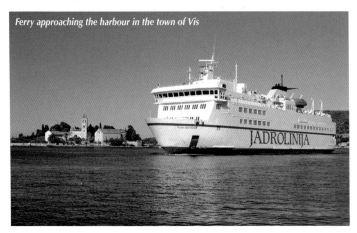

Ferry approaching the harbour in the town of Vis

ferry or catamaran, the most convenient ferry-departure points being Split, Zadar and Rijeka (see Appendix B). Services between some of the major islands are not as comprehensive as they might be (in some cases inter-island services are non-existent). Ferry tickets are cheap (sometimes an absolute bargain) for those travelling on foot, but less so for those with a car. As well as the larger passenger ferries (which also carry cars) there are smaller car ferries, small passenger-only ferries and faster passenger-only catamaran services.

Most routes are operated by the state ferry company Jadrolinija (www.jadrolinija.hr), and these are augmented by routes operated by a handful of smaller, private companies. Sailings vary from once daily to more than a dozen times a day, and are usually reduced out of season and over the winter (with some routes only operating during the summer). Book tickets for high-speed catamaran services at least a day in advance if possible (although sometimes ticket offices open only around half an hour before departures).

See the introduction to each island chapter for details of ferry routes from the mainland and other islands. For a complete list of ferry and catamaran services relevant to the walks in this guide, see Appendix C.

Flights

Croatia Airlines (www.croatiaairlines. com) operates flights between Zagreb and the cities of Pula, Rijeka (airport on the island of Krk), Zadar, Split and Dubrovnik on the coast. Fares are reasonable, and in all cases shuttle buses operate between the airport and city centre.

By train

There are regular rail services between Zagreb and Rijeka (4hrs) and Zagreb and Split (6hrs 30mins) – but no rail services along the coast itself, on the islands or between Zagreb and Dubrovnik. Rail fares are cheap in Croatia, and services reliable, although the high-speed train to Split is not as high-speed as might be expected (and suffered a major derailing in 2009). Faster, intercity trains are called *brzi vlak*; slower, local trains are called *putnički vlak*.

Buy tickets in advance (it costs more to pay on the train, and during the summer seats get booked up, especially the high-speed train to Split). Seat reservations are compulsory for international services and the high-speed service to Split, but not for local trains (note that if buying a return ticket, the seat reservation will be for the outward journey only – you'll still need to make a seat reservation for the return journey at the departure station for that part of your journey). A return (*povratna karta*) is cheaper than two singles, and two people travelling together can get a joint ticket (*zajednička karta*) at a reduced price (but there's only one ticket and you'll both have to travel together for the full journey including the return). See www.hznet.hr for timetables and fares (click on 'HŽ Putnički prijevoz', then select language, then click on 'timetables').

By bus

Local bus services operate on most of the major islands (including all but one of those featured in this guide) and in most cases provide a convenient, easy way to get around, at least between the main settlements. Some bus services connect neighbouring islands joined by a road bridge (for example, Cres and Lošinj), and continue to cities on the mainland via ferry (for example, buses from Cres cross by ferry to the island of Krk and continue from there to Rijeka and Zagreb on the mainland via road bridge).

Intercity buses cover most towns in Croatia and tend to be slightly more expensive than an equivalent train journey, while Croatia's new motorway system, constructed over the past decade, has cut journey times between Zagreb and the coast to similar to (or in most cases faster than) the equivalent route by train.

As with train tickets, return journeys are cheaper than two singles, and a return ticket on intercity routes includes a seat reservation only for the outward journey, so you'll need to pay for the return seat reservation once at your destination. There are no seat reservations on most short local routes. (Many ticket offices will tell you that a seat reservation for the return journey is not necessary, and often they'll be right, but it is advisable to politely insist that in your case it is necessary, rather than risk missing a connecting ferry or flight should all the seats suddenly get booked up).

See the introduction to each island chapter for details of local bus

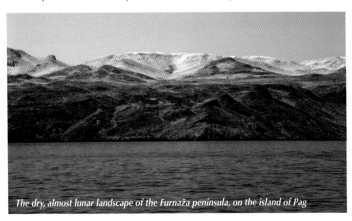
The dry, almost lunar landscape of the Furnaža peninsula, on the island of Pag

routes. For timetables and fares see www.autotrans.hr (covering many of the islands) and local tourist information office websites (details below, in the introduction to each island); otherwise try www.autobusni-kolodvor. com, although this never lists all services. For routes to/from Zagreb also check www.akz.hr.

By car

When driving in Croatia, whether in your own or a hire car, be aware of the following rules and regulations.

* Drive on the right and carry a driving licence at all times.
* Speed limits are 50km/h in towns or any other built-up areas, 90km/h on the open road, 110km/h on dual carriageways, and 130km/h on motorways (and for drivers under the age of 24, the speed limits are 10km/h less than each of these figures).
* Wearing seat belts is mandatory (including all passengers), as is the use of child seats for infants up to the age of six (children under 12 cannot sit in the front seat).
* Headlights must be switched on at all times, including (dipped) during the day.
* All cars must carry a reflective vest or jacket (which should be worn at the scene of an accident) and snow chains during the winter.
* Driving while using a mobile phone is prohibited.

* The blood alcohol limit is 0.05% (zero for drivers under the age of 24).

Motorways operate on a toll system, as does the bridge between the mainland and the island of Krk and the Učka Tunnel in Istria. Note that ferry prices for taking a car to the islands are much higher than for those travelling as foot passengers – another reason to use public transport. Drivers should note that the main coastal highway (Magistrala) is single lane, windy and gets extremely busy in the summer. In case of a breakdown, contact the Croatian Automobile Club (www.hak.hr, tel. 987).

Cycling

Croatia's islands are great for cycling. Traffic is in most cases less manic than on the coast, the views are often wonderful, and most tourist centres of any size have at least one place where you can hire bikes. Several local tourist boards have made a concerted effort to promote cycling, with maps of cycle routes available and some degree of signposting. There's also a national 'bed and bike' scheme, see www.mojbicikl.hr/bike-bed/.

Some of the best areas on the islands for cycling are the Kalifron peninsula on Rab; the Kabal peninsula and Stari Grad Plain on Hvar; the central part of Brač; the Bradat peninsula on Korčula; and Mljet. For more information on cycling in Croatia (including route descriptions for several islands, plus links to maps and

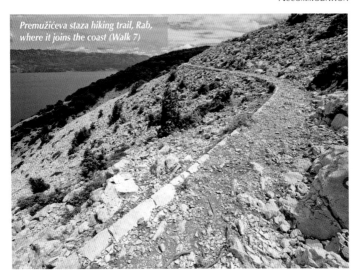

Premužićeva staza hiking trail, Rab, where it joins the coast (Walk 7)

other publications) see www.pedala. hr (website only partly in English; for routes click on 'biciklističke rute', then 'regije', where you can search by region).

Hitchhiking

Hitching on the Croatian coast and islands is generally a rather unsatisfying experience – few people are likely to stop, and it's not always easy to find a good place to stand where you're not going to get mown down by passing traffic. You can also try looking for a ride (with a small charge) on the local hitching forum, www.gorivo. com. In Croatia, as elsewhere, hitching can never be recommended as entirely safe for those travelling alone, particularly women.

ACCOMMODATION

There is a wide range of accommodation on the Croatian coast and islands – from large resort-style complexes to small boutique hotels, pensions (*pansion*), private rooms and apartments, hostels and campsites – and even several lighthouses. Private rooms (*sobe* – similar to a B&B, but usually without breakfast) and apartments (*apartmani* – usually with a small kitchen) are generally better value than hotels. Some rooms and apartments have a minimum one-week stay, and most will charge a supplement for stays less than three nights. Local tourist offices usually have private accommodation listed on their website, and some will book it for you, while others will refer you to a local agency for the booking

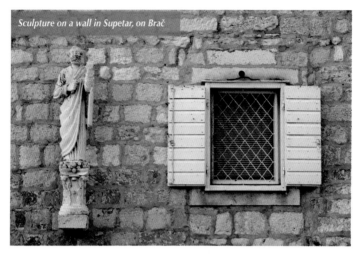
Sculpture on a wall in Supetar, on Brač

itself. In most cases the owner of the *soba* or *apartman* will come to meet you at the tourist office and show you to your chosen accommodation.

Hotels usually offer their best rates online. Try to book as far in advance as possible during the peak season (July–August), as places do get booked up. Prices are significantly lower during shoulder seasons (May–June and September–October), and many places close during the winter months (those which remain open tend to reduce their rates by as much as 50 per cent at this time). Prices are often quoted in euro and converted to kuna according to the daily rate. Hotels often only charge a small amount above their room rates for half-board. Wild camping, and camping within a national park or nature park, is prohibited.

A useful website to search for private rooms and apartments is www.gdjenamore.com. For youth hostels, see www.hfhs.hr; for lighthouses offering accommodation, see www.lighthouses-croatia.com. Local tourist board websites are listed in the introduction to each island.

FOOD AND WINE

Croatian food is delicious, and it's worth coming here just to eat.

Perhaps not surprisingly, seafood features prominently on menus on the islands, from 'premium' white fish such as gilthead bream (*orada*) and sea bass (*brancin*), which are priced by the kilo, to a wide array of shellfish and more humble but no less delicious dishes like marinated sardines. Fish is typically served grilled (*na žaru*) or boiled (*kuhano*), topped with olive oil, garlic and parsley, and traditionally served with *blitva* (Swiss chard) and potatoes.

Ispod peke is a slow, traditional Croatian method of cooking octopus, lamb or other meat – together with potatoes, onions, wine, olive oil and other ingredients – by roasting it in a shallow dish which is covered with an iron 'lid' or 'bell' sprinkled with hot coals.

Lamb is another perennial favourite on the islands, usually spit roasted or cooked *ispod peke* (the best lamb is said to come from the island of Pag, where the animals graze on sparse herbs dusted with sea spray by the bura wind).

Other traditional dishes to look out for on the islands include *pašticada* (a wonderfully opulent Dalmatian speciality, consisting of marinated beef or veal cooked slowly with dried plums, and typically served with home-made gnocchi and parmesan cheese); *brodet* (mixed fish stew, similar to Italian *brodetto*); *salata od hobotnice* (octopus and potato salad, with parsley, onion, garlic and olive oil); *hobotnica na žaru* (octopus roasted in the oven in its own juices, with potatoes, onions and olive oil); *rižoto od sipe* (cuttlefish risotto, black and cooked in its own ink); *punjene lignje* (stuffed squid); and chick pea (*slanutak*) stew, a traditional dish on Lastovo, usually served with marinated sardines. *Pršut* (Dalmatian prosciutto) is also served widely as an entrée. Istria, the wedge-shaped peninsula at the head of the Adriatic, is deservedly famous for its truffles (*tartufi*), and these are found on some menus on the islands too.

Pasta dishes are easy to find, and pizzerias are common and usually good, especially those with a wood-fired oven (*krušna peć*); 'pizza cut' is vastly inferior and best avoided! There's also plenty of snack food – try *bučnica*, a delicious pastry filled with courgette and cheese; *soparnik*, a pastry filled with Swiss chard; and *viška pogača*, an anchovy- and olive-filled pastry which is a speciality of the island of Vis. You'll often find a vast array of cakes, and the ice cream (*sladoled*) is truly heavenly (particularly in Zadar).

More restaurants are offering vegetarian options these days. If in doubt, ask 'Imate li nešto bez mesa?' ('Do you have something without meat?') or say 'Ja sam vegetarijanac' (men) or 'Ja sam vegetarijanka' (women), meaning 'I'm vegetarian'.

Any reasonably sized town has a market (*pijaca* or *tržnica*) selling items such as fresh fruit and vegetables, and local cheeses (the most famous cheese in Croatia is *Paški sir* from the island of Pag), and there are plenty of bakeries (*pekarnica*) selling bread as well as strudel and various other pastries. Croatian olive oil is excellent.

Croatian restaurants come in several guises – *restoran* (restaurant), *konoba* (slightly more homely and low key than a restaurant, although this is absolutely no indication of a drop in quality – possibly quite the

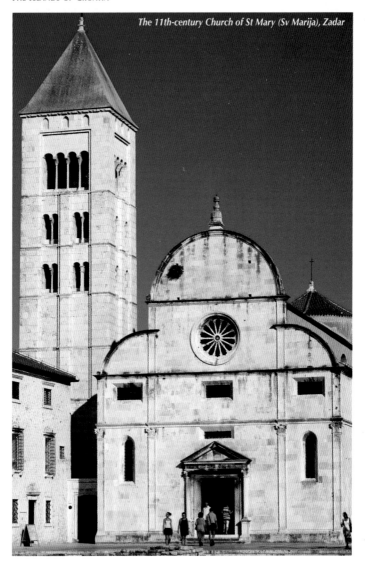

The 11th-century Church of St Mary (Sv Marija), Zadar

opposite), and *gostionica* (generally a more simple version of a konoba).

Croatia makes a lot of wine. Whites from the islands to look out for are Grk (from Korčula), Vugava viška (from Vis) and Žlahtina (from Krk); the best reds are made from the Plavac mali grape, with notable areas for the production of red wine being Ivan Dolac (on Hvar) and Dingač (on the Pelješac peninsula). The best Croatian beers are Karlovačko and Ožujsko (from Karlovac and Zagreb respectively) and the often elusive Velebitsko pivo.

VISAS

Croatia's entry requirements for most western nationals were relaxed even before it joined the EU in July 2013. Visas are unnecessary for visitors from most western countries. For example, a UK passport holder can enter the country for up to three months at a time. After this, it is necessary either to cross over the border into a neighbouring country before returning or to go through the lengthy process of applying for an extended-stay permit. Visitors are still officially required to register with the police within 48 hours of arrival, although if you are staying in hotels, private accommodation, mountain huts or official campsites this is automatically done for you when you hand your passport over to the agency, reception or hut warden. For more information on entry formalities see the website of the Croatian Ministry of Foreign Affairs (www.mvp.hr).

MONEY

The Croatian unit of currency is the kuna (abbreviated kn or HRK). The kuna comes in small coin denominations (currently 1, 2 and 5 kuna) and larger notes (currently 10, 20, 50, 100, 200, 500 and 1000 kuna, although the latter is less common). One kuna is comprised of 100 *lipa* (with coins in denominations of 5, 10, 20 and 50 lipa). When changing money, try to get a decent supply of smaller notes (20kn, 50kn and 100kn), as the larger notes can be hard to change in smaller shops and supermarkets.

ATMs (*bankomat*) are widespread in the larger towns and cities and major tourist centres, although don't expect to find one in smaller towns and villages. Currency is best changed at an exchange office (*mjenjačnica*), which will involve less queuing than in a bank. Rates should be displayed at the counter.

At the time of writing £1=9.1kn, €1=7.5kn, US$1=5.6kn. A number of prices (particularly accommodation) may be quoted in euros, which will then be converted into kuna according to the daily rate.

Although Croatia joined the EU in 2013, at the time of writing there is currently no official target date for adopting the Euro as currency.

Business hours

Shops in Croatia are generally open 08.00–20.00 Monday–Friday, with some closing earlier on Saturday,

Jadrolinija building, Rijeka

and most being closed on Sunday. Supermarkets are open longer hours, often 07.00–21.00 Monday–Saturday, and 08.00–15.00 Sunday. Cafés often open at 06.30. Markets are usually open 07.00–14.00 or similar. Shops and banks are closed on public holidays, but larger supermarkets will sometimes be open.

PHONE AND INTERNET

The international dialling code for Croatia is 00 385. Area codes include:

- **01** Zagreb
- **051** Rijeka (including Cres, Lošinj, Krk, Rab and other Kvarner islands)
- **023** Zadar (including Pag, Ugljan, Dugi otok and

CROATIAN NATIONAL HOLIDAYS

- 1 January (New Year's Day)
- 3 February (St Blaise's Day)
- Easter
- 1 May (Labour Day)
- Corpus Christi (60 days after Easter Sunday)
- 22 June (Day of Antifascist Struggle)

- 25 June (Statehood Day)
- 5 August (Homeland Thanksgiving Day)
- 15 August (Assumption of the Virgin Mary)
- 8 October (Independence Day)
- 1 November (All Saints' Day)
- 25 and 26 December (Christmas)

other northern Dalmatian islands)
- **022** Šibenik (including the Kornati islands)
- **021** Split (including Brač, Hvar, Vis and other central Dalmatian islands)
- **020** Dubrovnik (including Pelješac, Korčula, Lastovo, Mljet and other southern Dalmatian islands)

If calling Croatia from overseas, omit the initial zero from these area codes. Mobile phones work fine in Croatia, including in mountain areas, but not in areas of heavy forest cover. Those making a lot of calls or staying for a long period of time might consider buying a local SIM card (VIP, T-Mobile and Tele-2 are some of the main service providers), which will work out much cheaper for local calls (if your phone is locked and won't accept a new SIM card, new handsets are available from around 100kn).

Call boxes are found in post offices and are the cheapest way of calling overseas. Otherwise, phone cards are available from newspaper kiosks for use in public phone boxes, although these will not last particularly long on an international call.

Internet cafés are common in larger towns and cities, and most hotels and many private rooms and apartments these days have free wifi.

WATER

Tap water in Croatia is perfectly safe to drink. Bottled mineral water is widely available, but recycling

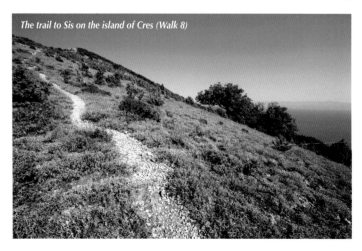

The trail to Sis on the island of Cres (Walk 8)

bins for plastic are not always to be found on the islands (although glass and sometimes plastic bottles can be returned to the supermarket). Non-recycled plastic will almost certainly go into landfill – an ongoing problem compounded by the high number of tourists visiting the islands. Consider whether it's really necessary to buy bottled water.

WALKING ON THE CROATIAN ISLANDS

Trail markings

Almost without exception, hiking trails in Croatia are clearly marked with a uniform system of waymarkings. Known locally as *markacija*, they are painted in red and white on trees, rocks or any other conspicuous object:

Trail markings

○ Simply indicates that you are on a marked trail of some sort. Adjacent signs or names of topographic features (again painted on trees and rocks) let you know exactly which path you are following.

❙❙ Indicates that the relevant trail continues straight ahead.

⟨⟨ Indicates a change in direction: not necessarily at a junction.

The first of these signs with a cross through it usually indicates a wrong turn or disused path. Otherwise, a cross by itself usually indicates a junction. Blue, green and yellow paint are often used to indicate caves, sinkholes and other related features.

Trail markings are sometimes supplemented by signposts, and in a couple of areas on the islands a completely different set of markings has been adopted – most successfully around Baška on the island of Krk, where a set of clear, coloured trail markings corresponds with routes marked on the detailed free map of the area.

Maps

Many of the islands included in this guide are covered by an excellent new series of detailed hiking maps published by the Croatian Mountain Rescue Service (Hrvatska Gorska služba spašavanja, HGSS or simply GSS) at a scale of 1:20,000 or 1:25,000, with hiking trails clearly marked and contour lines drawn to 20m. These are now available in the UK from the excellent The Map Shop (www.themapshop.co.uk), and can be bought in Croatia from local tourist information offices on the islands themselves (and 'Iglu' sports shops in Split, Rijeka and Zagreb) for around 35kn each. The sheets relevant to this guide are as follows:

- **Lošinj and Unije (Walks 10–12)** Lošinj – Tourist and Trekking Map (HGSS, 1:25,000); available from

Start of the trail to Oštravica, Orljak and Veli vrh, on Dugi otok (Walk 16)

the tourist information office in Mali Lošinj

- **Dugi otok (Walks 16–18)** Dugi Otok – Tourist and Trekking Map (HGSS, 1:25,000); planned publication date 2014
- **Brač (Walk 19)** Brač Bike – Bike Tourist Map (HGSS, 1:45,000); available from the tourist information offices in Supetar and Bol
- **Hvar (Walks 20–21)** Hvar Tourist and Trekking Map (HGSS, 1:25,000) – Zapad (West) sheet; available from the tourist information office in Stari Grad. The accompanying Istok (East) sheet has not yet been published, but the reverse of the West sheet covers the whole island at 1:40,000
- **Vis (Walks 22–24)** Otok Vis Tourist and Trekking Map (HGSS, 1:20,000); available from the tourist information office in Vis
- **Korčula (Walks 25–27)** Korčula Tourist and Trekking Map (HGSS, 1:25,000) – 2 sheets, Istok (East) and Zapad (West); available from the tourist information offices in Vela Luka, Korčula and Blato
- **Lastovo (Walk 28)** Park prirode Lastovsko otočje – Tourist and Trekking Map (HGSS, 1:20,000); available from the tourist information office in Lastovo town

Detailed maps of hiking routes are increasingly published by some local tourist boards, and are available (usually free) from local tourist information offices, including:

- **Krk (Walks 1–4)** Baška Marked Tourist Footpaths (Baška Tourist Office, approx 1:30,000);

available free from the tourist information office in Baška

- **Rab (Walks 5–7)** Otok Rab – Biking and Trekking (Rab Tourist Office, 1:25,000); available free from the tourist information office in Rab

Another detailed series of hiking maps, on one of which the recommended map for Rab (above) is based, and also at a scale of 1:25,000 or 1:30,000, is published by SMAND (www.smand.hr). However, while covering most of the main hiking areas on the Croatian mainland, the series currently covers only two of the islands (although maps of other islands are planned):

- **Rab (Walks 5–7)** Otok Rab (sheet 20a, 1:25,000)
- **Cres (Walks 8–9)** Otok Cres (sheet 21a, 1:25,000/1:75,000)

Your best chance of finding the SMAND sheets in Croatia is in one of the larger bookshops in a city such as Zagreb, Rijeka, Split or Zadar, rather than on the islands themselves; in the UK they are also stocked by the The Map Shop.

Other recommended maps are as follows:

- **Pag (Walks 13–14)** Island Pag Trekking and Mountain Biking; available free from the tourist information office in Pag town, although the scale of this is really too small for hiking purposes and the map is more geared towards cyclists
- **Ugljan (Walk 15)** Island Ugljan Map – Olive's island (approx 1:28,000); available free from the tourist information office in Preko. The same map covers Pašman on the reverse, in similar detail
- **Dugi otok (Walks 16–18)** Javna ustanova park prirode Telašćica

Tarin labyrinth in Tramuntana, Cres (Walk 9)

(1:25,000); available from the tourist information office in Sali

• **Mljet (Walks 29–30)** National Park 'Mljet' Traveler's Map (1:14,000); available from National Park offices on Mljet

Other relevant maps are listed in the introduction to each island.

For general planning purposes, any of the several maps available of Croatia will suffice – the free one produced by the Croatian National Tourist Board and available at tourist information offices all over the country can be recommended. There is a series of maps published by Freytag & Berndt covering the Croatian coast in a number of sheets (1:100,000). However, these do **not** accurately represent hiking trails and are primarily aimed at those planning a sailing holiday, so are really not at all useful.

DGU (Državna geodetska uprava) 1:25,000 maps are available for viewing online at http://geoportal. dgu.hr/viewer/?baselayer=HOK (tick 'Topografske karte TK25' in the left-hand panel and zoom in to the area you want to look at; if you want to buy the maps, they're 300kn per sheet).

Water

This being karst country, all rainwater rapidly disappears underground. That means there are no surface streams or reliable springs on these island walks – so carry enough water to last for the day.

Forest fires

Croatia's hot, dry climate makes forest fires a real danger, particularly during the summer, and visitors should be particularly aware of the threat they pose to the environment. Often caused by a carelessly discarded cigarette, fires spread rapidly and can burn for a considerable time before being brought under control, destroying huge tracts of landscape in the process. Never light an open fire, and exercise caution and common sense in the use of gas and multi-fuel stoves.

Heatstroke and dehydration

Hiking on the Croatian islands in July and August – particularly routes such as those on Pag, where there is nothing in the way of forest cover or shade – can mean extended exposure to relentlessly hot sun. Always make sure you carry sufficient water to avoid dehydration, a sunhat and sunscreen, and if possible avoid walking in the middle of the day.

Snakebites

Croatia has two venomous snakes, the Common viper or adder (as found in the UK) and the Nose-horned viper (see 'Reptiles and amphibians'; page 23). Although snakes will usually bite only in self-defence (when you step on, or too near, them), if snakebite does occur immobilise the limb or affected area, keep it below heart level, and get the victim to a doctor. Anti-venoms are available from hospitals and medical centres; sucking the wound and spitting has been shown to be completely ineffective. If possible try to identify the snake in question, but take care to avoid getting bitten yourself.

Strong currents

The Croatian coast is lovely for swimming, with some of the cleanest waters of the Adriatic being found off the Croatian islands, and the majority of beaches are very safe for swimming. However, be aware that at some of the more remote or less sheltered places, currents may be quite strong, which may make some such spots unsuitable for young children.

Unexploded ordnance

Unlike walking in some of the areas on the Croatian mainland, hiking on the islands does not bring the walker close to areas suspected of landmine deployment from the 1991–1995 war. However, bear in mind that two of the islands (Vis and Lastovo) have been used as military or naval bases in the past (Tito's headquarters during the Second World War were on Vis), and be alert for any sign warning of possible danger. If travelling in mainland Croatia look out for signs reading *opasnost!* (danger!), *mine* (landmines), *ne prilazite* (do not approach), *napušteni vojni objekt* (abandoned military installation) – all warnings you should take very seriously. However, there are no such dangers on the routes in this guide. It's worth recording that several years ago a tourist walking in the hills on the island of Vis (not on a marked trail) was seriously injured when he stood on a Second World War landmine.

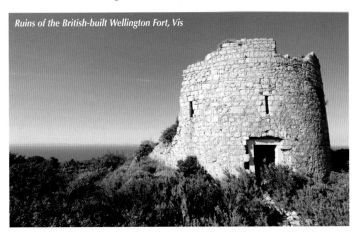
Ruins of the British-built Wellington Fort, Vis

WHAT TO DO IN AN EMERGENCY

Emergency phone numbers
- **92**   Police
- **93**   Fire
- **94**   Ambulance
- Emergency services can also be contacted on **112**

Hiking on the Croatian islands is generally easy and never too far from towns and villages, so the chances of requiring assistance from the Croatian Mountain Rescue Service (Hrvatska Gorska služba spašavanja, HGSS or simply GSS) are slim. Should you do so, however, the GSS has contact details of local offices listed on its website (www.gss.hr). The main units are on the mainland, including:

- Rijeka   +385 (0)91 721 0000
- Split   +385 (0)91 721 0001
- Zadar   +385 (0)91 721 0010
- For a full list of contacts see www.gss.hr/en/in-case-of-an-emergency.htm.

Like many such organisations around the world, the GSS provides free mountain rescue, but relies on the efforts and bravery of a small group of dedicated volunteers, whose services should not be called upon lightly.

Emergency state medical treatment in Croatia is effectively free to UK citizens, who need only pay a 10kn contribution to membership of health-care services if visiting a doctor (the same as Croatians pay), or 100kn per day (up to a maximum of 2000kn) for a stay in hospital. Note that this does **not** include private medical treatment, including visits to private GPs or dentists. The doctor, medical centre or hospital needs to be affiliated with the Croatian Health Insurance Fund (CHIF) – in Croatian, Hrvatski zavod za zdravstveno osiguranje (HZZO); www.hzzo.hr/en – so check this before-hand. Make sure you carry your passport and a European Health Insurance Card (EHIC) – search 'EHIC' at www.nhs.uk. As in the UK, non-emergency hospital treatment requires a referral from a GP. Medical and dental treat-ment in Croatia is of a very high standard.

Missing persons should be reported to the relevant embassy or consu-late (see Appendix F).

USING THIS GUIDE

Difficulty and arrangement of routes

The routes in this guide are arranged by island, starting in the north of the country and heading roughly south-east along the coast, rather than in any particular order of difficulty or duration. A short summary of the terrain and any particular difficulties encountered on a route is given in the box at the beginning of each walk, rather than each route having a grade to indicate difficulty. All the routes follow established trails, the majority of them clearly waymarked.

While a moderate level of fitness is assumed, the walks in the guide are in general very easy – none requires any scrambling/climbing skills or equipment, and the amount of ascent, the duration and the distances involved are moderate. However, heat from the sun in mid-summer, sudden changes in weather and/or strong winds (the bura) can make them seem considerably more challenging.

Timings and distances

The timing given in the box preceding each route description refers to an average walking speed, and does not include breaks or stopping time (as a general rule of thumb, add 10mins to every hour). Times and distances given in the box refer to the totals for that walk (so for a 'there-and-back' route they refer to both directions, not just one way). Altitudes and distances are given in metres and kilometres throughout the guide, and distances have been rounded to the nearest 0.5km.

Maps

The maps in this book have been prepared using the most detailed sources available, usually (where they exist) the hiking maps prepared by the HGSS, SMAND and/or local tourist boards, or maps produced by the Croatian State Geodetic Administration (DGU). It is recommended to obtain the HGSS maps and other listed sheets once in Croatia, to use in conjunction with this guide but in particular to explore areas of the islands not covered by the guide's routes. All route map extracts in this guide are printed at a scale of 1:25,000.

Several of the route maps used in this guide include their own numbered routes, which therefore appear on the guide's extracts. Note that these numbers do not correspond to the walk numbers in this book.

Spelling and local place names

English spelling has been used throughout this guide for the names of Croatian regions and surrounding countries (so 'Croatia' rather than 'Hrvatska'; 'Dalmatia' as opposed to 'Dalmacija'). Where discrepancies in the spelling of place names exist between the maps and route descriptions, these are listed in the information box at the start of each walk.

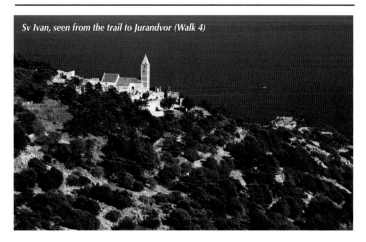
Sv Ivan, seen from the trail to Jurandvor (Walk 4)

One of the two largest islands on the Croatian Adriatic, Krk sits at the head of the Kvarner Bay, connected to the mainland by a long (1.4km) concrete double arch bridge called Krčki most, one of the longest such constructions in Europe. The bridge, and the island's proximity to Zagreb, make it one of Croatia's most popular holiday spots, in particular the small town of Baška, in the southeast of the island, with its 1800m arc of fine golden shingle, the enormously popular Vela plaža. The other main towns on the island are Krk town and Punat, on the southwest coast; the area around Vrbnik on the east coast is well known for its white wine, Žlahtina.

Baška lies at one end of a valley, enclosed on either side by high ridges,

the tops of which are a moonscape of shattered rock, scattered with clusters of *mrgari* – groups of ancient drystone-wall enclosures built to allow shepherds to count the sheep in collective flocks and sort/separate them into groups according to ownership based on their markings. Many of these mrgari are still in use. Baška has possibly the best-developed network of hiking trails of any of the islands – some 90km in total, well marked and well maintained, and passing through some outstanding scenery. Walkers could easily spend several days here without exhausting them. (Several small metal stamps (*žig*) with letters of the Glagolitic alphabet have been placed at various points on the routes around Baška, usually embedded into

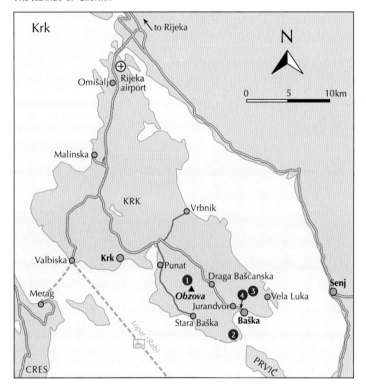

a rock at a summit or other point of interest – carry a small inkpad if you want to 'collect' these.)

Krk was inhabited during the Neolithic period (including a cave at Draga Bašćanska, near Baška), and there are the remains of several Illyrian hillforts on the island. During the Roman period the town of Krk (known as Curicum) became one of the most heavily fortified Roman towns on the eastern Adriatic, and a major sea

battle took place off the island in 49BC between Julius Caesar and Pompey.

Krk was a Venetian possession from 1001 and remained so until the arrival of Napoleon, although for many years a local dynasty, the Frankopans, ruled the island under only nominal Venetian suzerainty. The Venetians called the island Veglia.

It was on Krk that the so-called Baška Tablet (Bašćanska ploča) – a limestone tablet bearing one of the earliest inscriptions in the Croatian language written in the Glagolitic script – was discovered in the 19th century. Dating from AD1100, it was found in the floor of the small Church of Sv Lucija (St Lucy) in Jurandvor, a village on the outskirts of Baška. A copy of the tablet is on display in the church (Walk 4).

TOURIST INFORMATION

The tourist information office in Baška is in the old town (Kralja Zvonimira 114; tel. +385 (0)51 856 817; www.tz-baska.hr).

GETTING THERE AND GETTING AROUND

The main access point is the bridge, Krčki most, on which a toll is payable when driving towards the island, but not when leaving.

A car ferry plies the waters between Valbiska, on the west side of the island, and Merag, on the island of Cres (www.jadrolinija.hr). There is no longer a ferry between Baška and Lopar on Rab, unfortunately – the ferry now runs between Valbiska and Lopar (www.lnp.hr), which is less convenient for those based in Baška who are not driving (from Baška you'd need to take a bus to Malinska, then a bus to Valbiska, then wait for a ferry – buses aren't timed to connect with this line).

There's a regular bus service between Baška and Malinska, calling at the towns of Punat and Krk, and buses run from Baška to Rijeka, Zagreb and elsewhere on the mainland via the bridge (including several direct lines), as well as from Malinska to Merag on Cres, continuing to Cres town and the island of Lošinj (Walks 10 and 11). Note that buses will not always stop to pick up 'new' foot passengers when they drive off the ferry – and there are

Mrgari and large cairns on the slopes of Hlam (Walk 3)

no other local buses just to/from the ferry ports (Valbiska on Krk, Merag on Cres) apart from the inter-island services mentioned above, so breaking a journey at either Valbiska or Merag is not recommended.

Rijeka's international airport is actually on Krk, at Omišalj, in the north of the island, which is served by Croatia Airlines and several budget airlines (www.rijeka-airport.hr). Buses running between Malinska and the mainland via Krčki most bridge stop in Omišalj, and there's a shuttle bus service from the airport to Rijeka.

ACCOMMODATION

The Tamaris (www.baska-tamaris. com) towards the south end of the beach at Baška is one of the nicest hotels in the town. Private accommodation in Baška can be booked through Primaturist (www.primaturist. hr) and several other agencies (see www.tz-baska.hr).

MAPS

Baška Marked Tourist Footpaths (Baška Tourist Office, approx 1:30,000), available free from the tourist information office in Baška. Trail markings on the ground differ from the standard red-and-white 'bull's-eye' *markacije* – instead there are numbered and colour-coded trails, with signposts and other trail markings on the ground matching the numbered and colour-coded routes shown on the map, making route finding extremely clear.

OTHER ESSENTIALS

There are facilities such as ATMs, supermarkets and pharmacies in Baška's old town and along the busy promenade by the beach, as well as several places to rent bikes. For information on climbing routes on the crags around Baška see www.climbinbaska. com.

Veli vrh, looking towards the towns of Krk and Punat and, in the bay, the small island of Košljun (Walk 1)

WALK 1
Obzova

Start	Sculpture of the Glagolitic letter 'A' (*slovo Glagoljice 'A'*), around 500m from Treskavac pass (290m)
Finish	Baška (0m)
Distance	19.5km
Time	5hrs 40mins
Terrain	Short section on asphalt and unsealed roads, then rocky path throughout. Several escape points from which to descend to the valley and shorten the route. No technical difficulties, but can be rough underfoot on plateau, where path is faint. Route is easy to follow in clear weather, but could be lost in low cloud or mist.
Highest point	Obzova (568m)
Maps	Baška Marked Tourist Footpaths (Baška Tourist Office, approx 1:30,000). Route corresponds with route 14 on map (Vaclavov grebenski put), with short section of route 1 and short extension at start to include Glagolitic sculpture.
Access	Regular bus service between Baška and Malinska, calling at Punat and Krk. Bus stop on Treskavac pass, but none at Glagolitic sculpture, although drivers will usually drop off (but not pick up) there (say 'Kod slova Glagoljice A').
Note	This walk is known as Vaclavov grebenski put – which you'll see on signs and maps.

A superb mountain walk, covering the entire length of the ridge west of Baška, including the peaks of Obzova – the highest point on the island – as well as Veliki Hlam, Brestovica and others, and crossing a moonscape of shattered rock with several mrgari. The route can be walked in the opposite direction, but this way is preferable as it finishes in Baška (rather than requiring a wait for a bus on Treskavac) and has less ascent. The large sculpture of the Glagolitic letter 'A' at the start is one of several sculptures of the Glagolitic alphabet around Baška, and alludes to the island of Krk's prominence as a centre of Glagolitic learning in the medieval period.

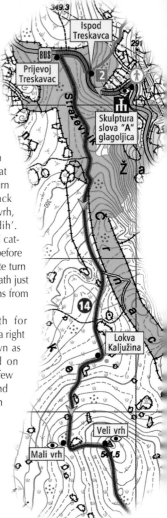

From the **sculpture** follow the main road uphill (care required – there's no pavement and there can be quite a bit of traffic) for 10mins to the bus stop on **Treskavac**, a saddle at 315m. ◀ From here turn left onto a 4WD track clearly marked 'Veli vrh, Obzova and Vratudih'. Pass the first gate and cattle grid, then shortly before reaching a second gate turn right onto a marked path just before a fence, 15mins from Treskavac.

For walkers following the route in reverse, note that buses don't stop to pick up at the sculpture, so backtrack to the official stop at Treskavac and wait for the bus there.

Follow the path for 10mins before taking a right fork (at a point known as Žičevo, not marked on the map) and then a few minutes later a second right fork, in both cases marked 'Veli vrh'. The path contours a rocky hillside with scattered juniper bushes and a few cairns, then snakes its way up to **Veli vrh** (541m).

The summit, surrounded by cairns, has good views of the town of Krk (northwest) and, just to the right of this, the tiny island of Košljun in the middle of a bay by the town of Punat; the island of Plavnik and the

Large sculpture of the Glagolitic letter 'A', near Treskavac

island of Cres (southwest) beyond; the prominent peak of Osoršćica on the island of Lošinj (southwest); and the Velebit mountains on the mainland (southeast).

Continue SSE towards Brestovica and Obzova, passing a

map continues on page 66

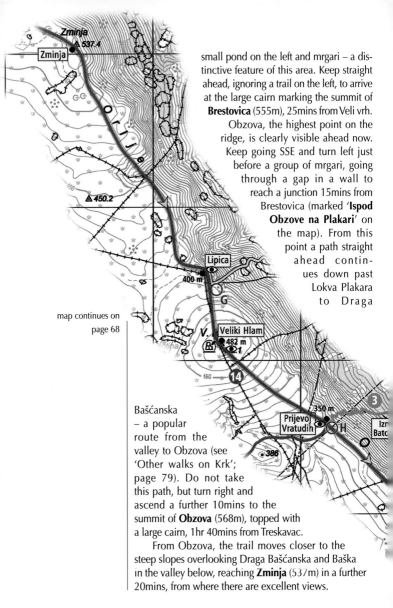

small pond on the left and mrgari – a distinctive feature of this area. Keep straight ahead, ignoring a trail on the left, to arrive at the large cairn marking the summit of **Brestovica** (555m), 25mins from Veli vrh. Obzova, the highest point on the ridge, is clearly visible ahead now. Keep going SSE and turn left just before a group of mrgari, going through a gap in a wall to reach a junction 15mins from Brestovica (marked '**Ispod Obzove na Plakari**' on the map). From this point a path straight ahead continues down past Lokva Plakara to Draga

map continues on page 68

Bašćanska – a popular route from the valley to Obzova (see 'Other walks on Krk'; page 79). Do not take this path, but turn right and ascend a further 10mins to the summit of **Obzova** (568m), topped with a large cairn, 1hr 40mins from Treskavac.

From Obzova, the trail moves closer to the steep slopes overlooking Draga Bašćanska and Baška in the valley below, reaching **Zminja** (537m) in a further 20mins, from where there are excellent views.

Continue along the ridge with a steep drop on the left, passing mrgari and a small pond before dropping down into a steep gully. Head through a gap in a wall and straight up the other side and bear right. Turn left alongside a wall and follow it round to the right, passing **Lokva Lipica** to reach **Veliki Hlam** (482m), 50mins from Zminja.

Bear left and go under a pylon to arrive in 20mins at **Vratudih**, a saddle at 350m, from where a trail descends steeply to Jurandvor and Baška on one side, and more gently to Stara Baška on the other. Keep straight ahead, passing a large cairn then going through a gap in a wall and bearing right, which leads to a superb viewpoint (marked '**Vrska glava**' on the map, but 'Vorganj' on the ground) with phenomenal views back along the entire ridge to Obzova.

After passing the junction with another trail from Jurandvor and Baška at **Bratinac** bear left to arrive at

Obzova, looking towards Brestovica and Veli vrh

67

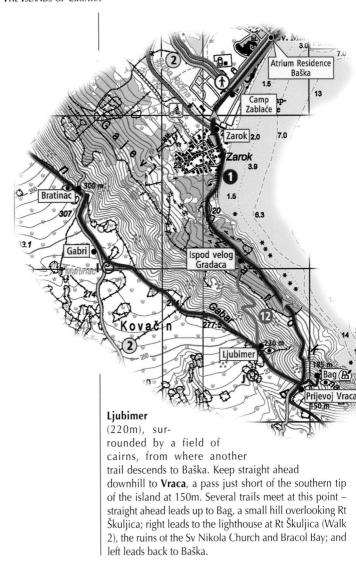

Ljubimer

(220m), sur-
rounded by a field of
cairns, from where another
trail descends to Baška. Keep straight ahead
downhill to **Vraca**, a pass just short of the southern tip
of the island at 150m. Several trails meet at this point –
straight ahead leads up to Bag, a small hill overlooking Rt
Škuljica; right leads to the lighthouse at Rt Škuljica (Walk
2), the ruins of the Sv Nikola Church and Bracol Bay; and
left leads back to Baška.

Turn left down a rocky trail to a gate, then through pine trees and along a cliff path above a nice little cove for swimming, and stride back down to the beach at **Baška**, a little over 2hrs from Vratudih.

The trail south of Vratudih, looking north from Vrska glava

WALK 2
Rt Škuljica

Start/Finish	Hotel Tamaris, Baška (0m)
Distance	6km
Time	2hrs
Terrain	Short and quite easy, but a bit steep just before Vraca, and fairly rocky on the way down to Rt Škuljica
Highest point	Bag (185m)
Maps	Baška Marked Tourist Footpaths (Baška Tourist Office, approx 1:30,000). Route corresponds with route 1 on the map.
Access	Regular bus service between Baška and Malinska, calling at Punat and Krk.

69

A short walk to Rt Škuljica, the headland south of Baška Bay, where there's a small lighthouse. The route can be extended to include a visit to the ruined Church of Sv Nikola and Bracol Bay, or added to the end of the longer, more challenging ridge walk from Treskavac (Walk 1).

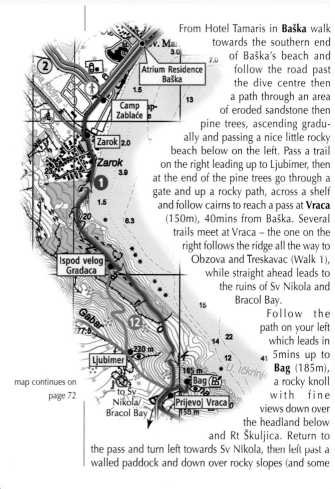

From Hotel Tamaris in **Baška** walk towards the southern end of Baška's beach and follow the road past the dive centre then a path through an area of eroded sandstone then pine trees, ascending gradually and passing a nice little rocky beach below on the left. Pass a trail on the right leading up to Ljubimer, then at the end of the pine trees go through a gate and up a rocky path, across a shelf and follow cairns to reach a pass at **Vraca** (150m), 40mins from Baška. Several trails meet at Vraca – the one on the right follows the ridge all the way to Obzova and Treskavac (Walk 1), while straight ahead leads to the ruins of Sv Nikola and Bracol Bay.

Follow the path on your left which leads in 5mins up to **Bag** (185m), a rocky knoll with fine views down over the headland below and Rt Škuljica. Return to the pass and turn left towards Sv Nikola, then left past a walled paddock and down over rocky slopes (and some

map continues on page 72

Rt Škuljica

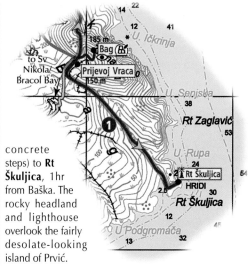

concrete steps) to **Rt Škuljica**, 1hr from Baška. The rocky headland and lighthouse overlook the fairly desolate-looking island of Prvić.

Return to **Baška** by the same route or, to make a slightly longer excursion, visit Sv Nikola and Bracol Bay.

WALK 3

Hlam

Start/Finish	Baška bus station (42m)
Distance	13km
Time	3hrs 15mins
Terrain	Easy for its first half, following a clear forest trail, then a little more rocky across the plateau, with a fairly steep descent
Highest point	Hlam (461m)
Maps	Baška Marked Tourist Footpaths (Baška Tourist Office, approx 1:30,000). Route corresponds with routes 7 and 11 on the map.
Access	Regular bus service between Baška and Malinska, calling at Punat and Krk.

Another excellent walk in the Baška area, passing the historic Church of Sv Ivan, then ascending on a lovely forest path to the 'lunar' landscape of the rocky plateau around Hlam, and descending via a steep gully. The route can be combined with Walk 4 to finish in Jurandvor.

From the bus station in **Baška** follow the road uphill, then turn right onto a track, cross the main road and walk uphill on an asphalt road towards Sv Ivan. Pass a trail on the left to Jurandvor and Hlam, then just after a hairpin bend turn right onto an

Ruin passed on the route up from Sv Ivan

unmarked path, which leads up to the car park just before the cemetery at **Sv Ivan**, 15mins from the bus station.

> **Sv Ivan** was the first parish church to be built in the valley, in the 11th century, but was abandoned at the beginning of the 19th century and subsequently restored. Its bell tower houses the oldest bell in the area (known as The Old Man), dating from 1431.

From the car park walk uphill past a stone ruin, on a lovely broad, well-engineered path through lush pine forest with the occasional well-placed bench to rest on. After three sharp corners the trail levels out through more scattered trees, and about 45mins from the church a faint trail is reached on the right opposite a bench. Turn right onto this trail, meandering through low trees and following blue triangles painted on rocks, then go over a wall to **Stražice** (371m), a lookout point with fantastic views.

Obzova and Veliki Hlam (both Walk 1) lie on the opposite side of the valley, and the rocky island to the southeast is Prvić, just off Rt Škuljica (Walk 2) at the tip of the southern headland of Baška Bay. To the southeast are Goli otok, with the northeast coast of Rab beyond, including Kamenica, and to the east and southeast the mountains of Northern Velebit run along the coast of the mainland above Senj.

> On the rocky slopes just to the east of Stražice are large groups of **mrgari** – clusters of ancient drystone-wall enclosures built to allow shepherds to count the sheep in collective flocks and separate them into groups according to ownership based on their markings.

Return to the main trail and turn right to reach a small rest area and information board before a wall in 5mins, which marks the edge of the so-called **Plato mjeseca** ('Lunar plateau') or Planina mjesec – a rock-strewn plateau with little vegetation, criss-crossed by drystone walls and clusters of mrgari. Walk through the gap in the wall onto this plateau, turn right, and then go through a gap in another wall and left onto a 4WD track. Go through a gate and turn left alongside the wall. Pass mrgari and a small pond (**Kalić lokva**), then follow large cairns up

View of the narrow channel between Rt Škuljica and the island of Prvić, from Hlam

Descending from Hlam towards Baška

the hillside to a gate. Go through this and up to reach the summit of **Hlam** (461m), 30mins from the edge of the plateau. It's a lovely airy spot, although the views from the summit itself are not quite as extensive as those from Stražice or the opposite side of the valley (Walk 1).

The trail to the right leads to Zakam, another good viewpoint, and the village of Jurandvor (Walk 4).

Descend by the same route, but just before reaching the rest area at the edge of the plateau go straight ahead instead of left, following the green trail markings down a steep rocky gully to reach a junction in 30mins. ◀ Turn left to reach the road from Baška up to Sv Ivan, and right onto this to return to the bus station in **Baška**.

WALK 4
Zakam and Jurandvor

Start	Baška bus station (42m)
Finish	Jurandvor (60m)
Distance	5km
Time	1hr 20mins
Terrain	Easy walking on good paths
Highest point	Zakam (194m)
Maps	Baška Marked Tourist Footpaths (Baška Tourist Office, approx 1:30,000). Route corresponds with route 6 on the map.
Access	Regular bus service between Baška and Malinska, calling at Punat and Krk.

An easy walk to the Church of Sv Lucija (St Lucy) in Jurandvor, where the so-called Baška Tablet was found – one of the most important historical finds in Croatia from the medieval period. The route avoids the main road and includes a great viewpoint overlooking Baška Bay, Zakam. This can be combined with Walk 3 for a longer, more challenging route.

From the bus station in **Baška**, follow the road uphill then turn right onto a track, cross the main road and

The Church of Sv Lucija (St Lucy) in Jurandvor, where the Baška Tablet was found

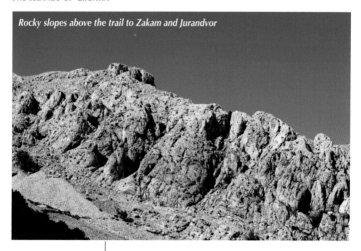
Rocky slopes above the trail to Zakam and Jurandvor

Alternatively, keep straight ahead here to follow Walk 3 and create a longer route.

If you miss it, just follow the road down and turn left just before the main road, then left again to arrive at the front of the church.

walk uphill on an asphalt road towards Sv Ivan, then turn left onto a trail to Jurandvor and Hlam. ◄ On reaching a junction keep straight ahead – the path on the right leads up to Hlam (Walk 3) – through a tunnel of trees, then take a right fork and walk uphill with imposing crags and cliffs above on the right. Turn left off the main trail to arrive at **Zakam** (194m), marked by a large cross, with views across the Bay of Baška and up to the Church of Sv Ivan (Walk 3).

Return to the main trail and turn left, following a nice shady path through tall pines, then going downhill through a gate on a stony trail to reach the houses of **Jurandvor**. A path on the left leads to the back of the Church of Sv Lucija. ◄

> **Sv Lucija** was built around the end of the 12th century on the remains of an earlier Christian church. It was in the floor of Sv Lucija that the Baška Tablet was discovered in the 19th century – a limestone tablet bearing one of the earliest inscriptions in the Croatian language written in the Glagolitic script, recording a donation of land to the church by the

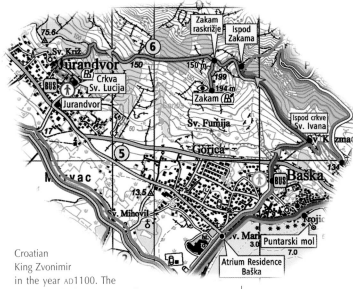

Croatian
King Zvonimir
in the year AD1100. The
version on display is a copy – the original is in the Croatian Academy of Arts and Sciences
in Zagreb. The church's main altar is decorated with
a 14th-century wooden polyptych (painting divided
into panels) by the sons of Paolo Veneziano.

Buses to Baška (or Krk, Punat, and so on) stop on the
main road in Jurandvor. Alternatively simply walk back
down the main road into **Baška** (allow 15mins).

OTHER WALKS ON KRK

Obzova from Draga Bašćanska

While Walk 1 includes Obzova, the highest point on
the island of Krk, those who want to follow a shorter
route to this peak can start from the village of Draga
Bašćanska (route 15 on the recommended map) and

follow a well-marked trail west from the church of Sv Rok. It climbs steadily up to the ridge and passes Lokva Plakara before joining Walk 1 just north of Obzova (allow up to 4hrs return). To vary the return, continue south on Vaclavov grebenski put (see Walk 1) to Vratudih, from where a steep but well-marked trail zigzags down to the village of Jurandvor. Both Draga Bašćanska and Jurandvor are on the bus route from Baška to Malinska, although if you're extending this route slightly and descending to the valley from Vratudih, Jurandvor is only a 15min walk from Baška.

Vela Luka
A trail leads northeast from Baška's old town (route 9 on the recommended map) to Vela Luka, a deep inlet and popular beach with several restaurants and cafés. The trail crosses a small canyon (Kanjon Vrženica raskrižje) and passes through an extensive group of mrgari at Lubinin. The ruins of the old Roman settlement of Corinthia lie just north of the beach at Vela Luka. It's possible to return to Baška from Vela Luka by taxi boat.

RAB

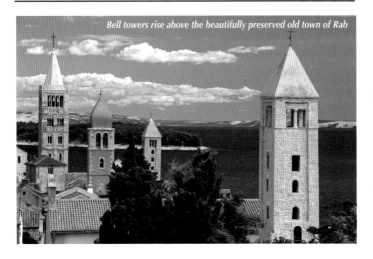
Bell towers rise above the beautifully preserved old town of Rab

Rab sits in the lee of its larger Kvarner neighbours, the islands of Krk and Cres, which encircle it to the north and west, while the finger-like tip of Pag's Lun peninsula lies to the south. Rab is less than 2km from the mainland at its southeast point. The steep rocky slopes of the island's east coast (Walk 6), including its highest point, Kamenjak (409m, Walk 5), face the magnificent Velebit mountains on the mainland across the narrow Velebitski kanal (Velebit channel) and provide the best views of these mountains from any of the islands. (Walks 5 and 6 can be combined with Walk 7 to create the finest walk on the island. Walk 7 itself follows one of three

'geopark' trails on Rab, which provide a series of clearly marked points of geological interest.)

The harsh landscape of the east coast, crisscrossed by drystone walls and exposed to the full force of the bura wind, quickly gives way to more gentle, greener landscapes further west, in particular the enormous Kalifron peninsula (see 'Other walks on Rab'; page 94), covered in lush pine trees and constituting one of the most heavily forested areas of any of the Adriatic islands. Part of Kalifron forms the Dundo Forest Reserve, which contains a large number of cork trees, and the whole peninsula is covered by a web of hiking and cycling trails, alive

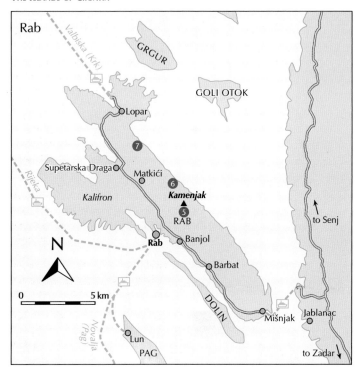

with scurrying lizards and butterflies and leading to secluded coves.

Rab town has a beautifully preserved old historic centre, clinging to a small peninsula on the eastern side of the harbour – a maze of narrow atmospheric stone streets, squares and alleyways lined with Romanesque, medieval, Venetian and Neo-Gothic architecture, its steep walls plunging into the sea and its skyline pierced by four elegant bell towers. Rab's Medieval Crossbow Tournament,

held in Rab town on 9 May, 25 June, 27 July (St Christopher's Day, the city's patron saint) and 15 August (Assumption Day), is well worth seeing. The tournament, which dates back to the 14th century and marks the successful defence of the city against a siege in 1358, was revived by the Rab Crossbowmen's Association (Udruga rapskih samostrelicara) in 1995. It is one of only two tournaments in the world using the medieval crossbow (the other is in San Marino in Italy)

– a heavy weapon which shoots a handcrafted wooden bolt at speeds of around 90m per second at a target the size of a small dinner plate.

TOURIST INFORMATION

The tourist information office in Rab town is on the main square, by the waterfront on the northeast side of the old town (Trg Municipium Arba 8; tel. +385 (0)51 724 064; www.tzg-rab.hr).

GETTING THERE AND GETTING AROUND

Rab town is served by a daily (during summer) catamaran service between Novalja (on the island of Pag) and Rijeka (www.jadrolinija.hr), arriving early in the morning from Novalja and departing for Novalja in the evening. (If you intend to travel onward from Novalja to Pag or Zadar be sure to check bus times during the early summer, as the summer timetable for the bus tends to start a few weeks after that of the catamaran, so it is possible to end up stuck in Novalja until the following morning.) A regular ferry connects Mišnjak in the northeast of the island with Jablanac on the mainland (www.jadrolinija.hr), and buses running between Rab town and Rijeka or Zagreb use this route (note that there's no other public transport between Rab and Mišnjak, and between Jablanac and the main coastal highway). However, anyone wanting to travel south (to Zadar, for example) really needs to go as far as Senj and take a bus south from there, as buses

Rab town

are unlikely to stop at the Jablanac turnoff on the main road, making it much less practical than taking the catamaran to Novalja. Another company does a similar crossing to the mainland, from Mišnjak and Stinica (www.rapska-plovidba.hr). There's also a ferry (www.lnp.hr) several times a day between Lopar in the northwest of the island and Valbiska (on the island of Krk), and a small passenger boat (daily during summer, www.rapska-plovidba.hr) between Rab town and Lun (on the island of Pag), although there is no onward public transport between Lun and Novalja (a taxi will cost around 200kn). Finally, some of the hotels on Rab run a shuttle service, depending on season and the number of passengers, from Zadar airport via Pag.

There's a good local bus service between Rab town and Lopar, via Barčići and Matkići, which covers the trailheads for Walks 5, 6 and 7 – timetables available at the bus station and tourist information office in Rab town (or see www.autotrans.hr). The bus station (for buses to Lopar, and for Rijeka and Zagreb via the Mišnjak–Jablanac ferry) in Rab town is a 5min walk northwest of the old town.

ACCOMMODATION

Private accommodation can be booked through Kristofor (www.kristofor.hr) and other agencies listed on the Rab Tourist Board website (www.tzg-rab.hr).

MAPS

Otok Rab – Biking and Trekking Map (Rab Tourist Office, 1:25,000), extracts of which illustrate the routes for Walks 5, 6 and 7 in this guide, is available free from the tourist information office in Rab town. Note that the gridlines on the map are not oriented north, whereas those on the SMAND map – Otok Rab (sheet 20a, 1:25,000), on which the free map is based – are oriented north. The small leaflet 'Geopark Rab: Premužićeva staza 1' (approx 1:24,000), also available free from the tourist information office, is also useful for Walk 7.

ESSENTIALS

There are ATMs, supermarkets and pharmacies in the old town. For bike hire the best place is Eros Rab (www.rab-novalja.com) on the Riva.

WALK 5

Kamenjak

Start/Finish	Bus station, Rab town (5m)
Distance	8km
Time	2hrs 30mins
Terrain	Road walking on asphalt for first half, then good clear trail. Easy walk, although proximity to Velebit (and its bura winds) means it shouldn't be attempted in bad weather.
Highest point	Kamenjak (409m)
Maps	Otok Rab – Biking and Trekking Map (1:25,000) (**note** the map/grid is not oriented north). SMAND Otok Rab (sheet 20a, 1:25,000)
Access	To avoid some of initial road walking, take Rab–Lopar bus from bus station in Rab town and ask to be dropped at Barčići by turnoff to Kamenjak (say 'Za Kamenjak'). Walk up road towards Pahlinići and start of path to Kamenjak (25mins).

A short, straightforward walk to Kamenjak (409m), the highest point on the island of Rab, passing a viewpoint with good views down over Rab town. The summit of Kamenjak itself is less inspiring, topped with huge telecommunications antennae in a fenced-off area. However, walking around to the far side of the antennae and continuing along the coast towards Lopar (see Walk 6 and Walk 7) instantly turns this into the finest walk on the island, with phenomenal views of Velebit. Some initial road walking is unavoidable unless you have your own car – but then you wouldn't be able to continue along the coast to Lopar.

From the bus station in **Rab town**, follow the road away from the old town, then take the first road on the right. A short distance up this road, at the point where it turns to the left, keep straight ahead to gain a broad stone path uphill. (Construction work in this area at the time of writing may make the route here less clear in future. If uncertain, just follow the road uphill and turn right to arrive at the point where the path meets the road again.) Rejoin the road at a

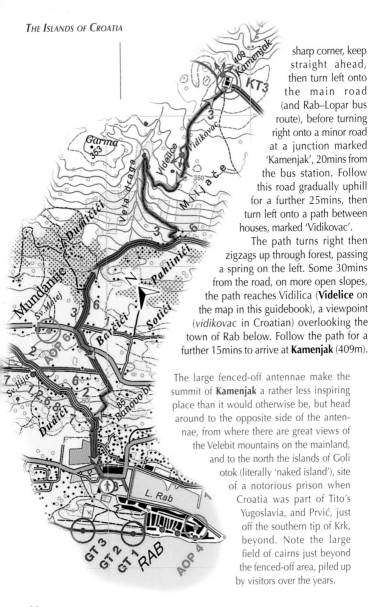

sharp corner, keep straight ahead, then turn left onto the main road (and Rab–Lopar bus route), before turning right onto a minor road at a junction marked 'Kamenjak', 20mins from the bus station. Follow this road gradually uphill for a further 25mins, then turn left onto a path between houses, marked 'Vidikovac'.

The path turns right then zigzags up through forest, passing a spring on the left. Some 30mins from the road, on more open slopes, the path reaches Vidilica (**Videlice** on the map in this guidebook), a viewpoint (*vidikovac* in Croatian) overlooking the town of Rab below. Follow the path for a further 15mins to arrive at **Kamenjak** (409m).

The large fenced-off antennae make the summit of **Kamenjak** a rather less inspiring place than it would otherwise be, but head around to the opposite side of the antennae, from where there are great views of the Velebit mountains on the mainland, and to the north the islands of Goli otok (literally 'naked island'), site of a notorious prison when Croatia was part of Tito's Yugoslavia, and Prvić, just off the southern tip of Krk, beyond. Note the large field of cairns just beyond the fenced-off area, piled up by visitors over the years.

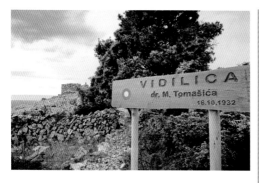

Vidikovac, a lookout point on the slopes of Kamenjak

There's a restaurant partway down the road to Rab town, although it's fairly out of the way and you'll have a wider choice back in Rab town.

▶ Descend to **Rab town** by the same route – or, a far better proposal, follow Walks 6 and 7 along the coast to Lopar.

WALK 6
Kamenjak to Matkići

Start	Kamenjak (409m)
Finish	Bus stop on main Rab–Lopar road by turnoff to Matkići (30m)
Distance	5km
Time	4hrs 40mins
Terrain	Route fairly faint in places but easy enough to follow; quite rocky with some boulder-hopping and one short, very slightly exposed section
Highest point	Kamenjak (409m)
Maps	The Island of Rab – Biking and Trekking Map (1:25,000) (**note** the map/grid is not oriented north). Leaflet 'Geopark Rab: Premužićeva staza 1' (approx 1:24,000) is useful for last part of route.
Access	See Walk 5 for route to Kamenjak. Bus between San Marino, Lopar and Rab picks up passengers at turnoff to Matkići – so return to Rab is possible from Matkići or Lopar (if this walk combined with Walk 7).

A spectacular route above the island's relentlessly rocky and rugged northeast coast, with unbeatable views of the Velebit mountains on the mainland. The route is best combined with Walks 5 and 7, thus creating a route from Rab town that climbs to Kamenjak then follows the northeast coast all the way to the Lopar peninsula. This section is on a faint although easy-to-follow trail (drystone wall on your left, and the sea on your right) with plenty of boulder-hopping.

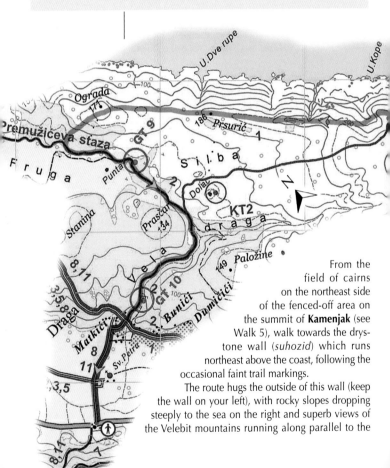

From the field of cairns on the northeast side of the fenced-off area on the summit of **Kamenjak** (see Walk 5), walk towards the drystone wall (*suhozid*) which runs northeast above the coast, following the occasional faint trail markings.

The route hugs the outside of this wall (keep the wall on your left), with rocky slopes dropping steeply to the sea on the right and superb views of the Velebit mountains running along parallel to the coast on the mainland. (This, the northernmost section of Velebit, contains Northern Velebit National Park.) The smallish rocky island more or less straight ahead to the north is Goli otok (literally 'naked island'), site of a notorious prison camp when Croatia was part of Tito's Yugoslavia. ▶ The long rocky spur beyond Goli otok is Prvić, an island off the southern tip of Krk, and the mountains on the mainland beyond are part of Gorski kotar and Velika kapela.

Most older politicians, including Croatia's former president Stjepan Mesić, did some time at the prison for 'disagreeing' with the then communist system.

About 45mins from Kamenjak the trail heads right downhill towards an old hut, then left around the hut before a barbed-wire fence – the trail here passes above some steep cliffs and is slightly exposed. Contour the slope (faint trail markings) rather than following the barbed-wire fence straight back up, then continue alongside the wall as before. ▶

The trail descends again slightly to the right, crossing two broken stone walls, the second of which has a bit of a drop on the far side, then goes uphill again to arrive at a ruined stone hut, 90mins from Kamenjak. Turn inland (NW) here and duck left through a gap in the wall, then go right (NE) through the first of two gaps in a wall. Follow faint trail markings uphill to regain the crest of the

Note the 'hole' in the wall blocked with branches – a simple gate to allow sheep in and out as required.

ridge above the coast again. Continue over a succession of broken walls and around the head of a steep gully to arrive at a junction 2hrs 50mins from Kamenjak, where a trail inland leads down to join Premužićeva staza (Walk 7). Instead, keep straight ahead on the trail marked 'grebenski put' ('ridge walk') and 'Lopar' – although rocky, it's really no more difficult than the route followed so far from Kamenjak, and is not exposed.

Pass a large cairn (**Prsurić**), then a stone shelter, and a prominent tree bent almost horizontal by the wind – this and other bent trees on the slopes below are a good indicator of the strength of the bura, the powerful northeasterly wind which sweeps across from Velebit, with gusts frequently reaching gale force.

A little over 30mins from the junction, before reaching another prominent cairn, turn left inland – the correct point to turn inland can be a bit hard to find, but involves crossing over a low wall (where there are trail markings) among some trees. From here the route is clear enough, downhill to reach a junction with **Premužićeva staza** in 5mins.

The route can be extended all the way to Lopar by turning right here and following the description in Walk 7.

◄ Turn left on Premužićeva staza, a nice, well-engineered track built by Ante Premužić, a Croatian forestry engineer, in the 1930s. (Premužić is best known for his other Premužićeva staza on Northern Velebit.)

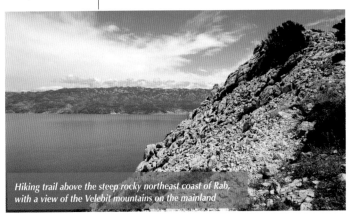

Hiking trail above the steep rocky northeast coast of Rab, with a view of the Velebit mountains on the mainland

Pass a prominent, mushroom-shaped rock (an erosional remnant), then a trail on the left leading up to the coast path you've just followed, then two retention dams (built to protect the valley from flash floods). After following Premužićeva staza for around 40mins, turn right onto an asphalt road, then go left downhill through the scattered houses of **Matkići** (passing a church on the left) to reach the main **Rab–Lopar road** by a church. Here walkers can flag down a passing bus back to Rab town.

WALK 7
Premužićeva staza (Matkići to Lopar)

Start	Bus stop on main Rab–Lopar road by turnoff to Matkići (30m)
Finish	Lopar (San Marino) (<5m)
Distance	8km
Time	2hrs 10mins
Terrain	Short sections on asphalt at either end of the route; otherwise broad, well-engineered track throughout
Highest point	140m
Maps	The Island of Rab – Biking and Trekking Map (1:25,000) (**note** the map/grid is not oriented north). Leaflet 'Geopark Rab: Premužićeva staza 1' (approx 1:24,000)
Access	Regular bus service between Rab and Lopar, leaving from bus station in Rab and returning from San Marino. Drops off and picks up by church at turnoff to Matkići (say 'Za Matkiće').

An interesting walk on a well-engineered historic trail (Premužićeva staza), including a spectacular section along the coast. This is one of three 'Geopark' trails on the island of Rab, with a series of clearly marked and labelled points of geological interest – from erosional remnants to fossilised gastropods. It can be combined with Walks 5 and 6 to make an outstanding day out, starting from Rab town, climbing to Kamenjak, and then following the island's spectacularly rugged northeast coast all the way to Lopar.

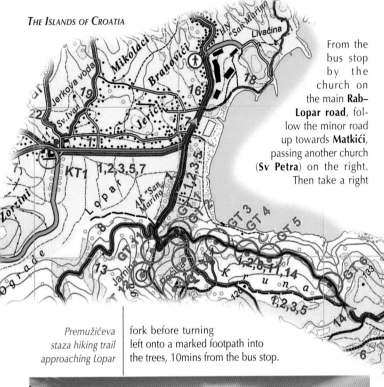

From the bus stop by the church on the main **Rab–Lopar road**, follow the minor road up towards **Matkići**, passing another church (**Sv Petra**) on the right. Then take a right

Premužićeva staza hiking trail approaching Lopar

fork before turning left onto a marked footpath into the trees, 10mins from the bus stop.

After 5mins, pass two retention dams on the right, built to protect Vela draga from flash floods, then after a further 20mins pass a distinctive mushroom-shaped erosional remnant. Pass a wooden cross and then a path on the right which leads up to Prsurić and the trail along the coast to Kamenjak (see Walk 6). Keep straight ahead on a brackeny path (not the broad 4WD track on the right), going under pylons and passing a large area of soil erosion on the left. At a junction 45mins from the start of the path go left and slightly downhill to a prominent group of karst rocks. Return to the previous junction and turn left, then after the pylons turn right onto a beautiful coastal trail, which winds its way gradually down towards Lopar, with wonderful views of Velebit.

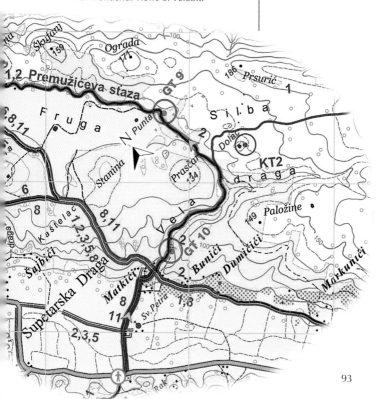

Several more **geological features** beside the trail are highlighted and explained, including gastropods and rudist fossils (extinct snails and marine bivalves respectively, from the Cretaceous Era, when this region was submerged beneath a warm, shallow sea), a solution pan, and a small former bauxite mine (bauxite is a component of aluminium ore and was mined here in the late 1920s).

Go over a bridge and then right through a gate, walking through a large campsite, then continue straight ahead on the main road to arrive at the bus stop in **San Marino** (Lopar), on the right.

OTHER WALKS ON RAB

Kalifron
The enormous wooded Kalifron peninsula near Rab town is one of the greenest areas on the Adriatic, and is covered by some 50km of hiking and biking trails. The distances, and the fact that many of the trails are 4WD tracks, make it a perfect area for cycling. For those who want to do a short walk on the peninsula, Premužićeva staza II, another of the paths built by forestry engineer Ante Premužić in the 1930s (see Walk 7), makes a good short hike. It is covered by a small free brochure and map available from the tourist office in Rab town.

Early morning in the harbour of Cres town

Cres is one of the two largest islands on the Croatian Adriatic, more or less equal in size to Krk at around 405km². Long and slender in the north, where it is separated by only a little over 4km from the Istrian coast, it stretches down alongside Krk, Rab and the northern tip of Pag, defining the western edge of the Kvarner islands.

Griffon vultures nest on the soaring sea cliffs of its northeast coast, near the village of Beli – the last remaining nesting area of these magnificent birds in Croatia. The highest point of the island is also in the north – usually given as Sis (639m) (Walk 8), although Gorice (648m) is a little higher – while the rugged area around Beli itself, known as Tramuntana, is traversed by a network of old forest trails linking a scattering of abandoned villages (Walk 9). The island's main town, Cres, is located on a deep bay on the western side of the island – an alluring place with plenty of narrow stone streets and old

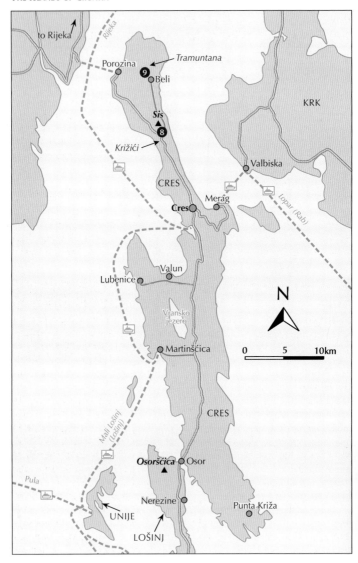

Venetian palazzi clustered around the pretty natural harbour. Further down the west coast of the island, Lubenice is a particularly beautiful little village with only a dozen or so inhabitants, perched on a cliff above a remote pebble beach, some 378m below. At the centre of the island is Vransko jezero, a large freshwater lake (a rare thing in these parts) which supplies water to the whole island as well as neighbouring Lošinj, while another high area rises above its western shore, Helm (487m).

Cres is separated from the neighbouring island of Lošinj by a narrow artificial channel, only 11m wide, thought to have been dug by the Liburnians some 3000 years ago. The two islands are linked at the town of Osor by road bridge, which swings aside to allow yachts and other small boats to sail through twice a day. Known as the Cavanelle, the channel was of enormous importance to shipping (Roman, early medieval and Venetian) on the Adriatic, since it allowed ships to follow a more sheltered route than that along the western shore of Lošinj.

Osor (ancient Apsorus, which rose to prominence during the late Bronze and early Iron Age) grew fantastically rich from its strategic position, remaining the island's capital until the 15th century, when Venice moved its administrative capital of the two islands to Cres town. With the advent of steam and associated changes in shipping routes the town went into a long, slow decline, exacerbated by malaria, plague and pirates. These days Osor has fewer than 65 inhabitants – although it still has the remains of town walls, a 15th-century cathedral, loggia and a bishop's palace to tell of its former glory – and, lately, a nice scattering of outdoor sculpture. Osor lies at one end of the excellent walk over Osoršćica just over the channel on Lošinj (Walk 10).

TOURIST INFORMATION

The tourist information office in Cres town is just off the waterfront, a 3min walk from the bus station (Cons 10; tel. +385 (0)51 571 535; www.tzg-cres.hr).

GETTING THERE AND GETTING AROUND

There are regular car ferry services between Porozina at the northern tip of the island and Brestova on the Istrian coast, and from Merag on the island's east coast to Valbiska on the island of Krk (both www.jadrolinija. hr), and a catamaran stops at Cres town itself on its route between Mali Lošinj (on Lošinj) and Rijeka (www. krilo.hr). Cres is connected by a short bridge to the neighbouring island of Lošinj, and the town of Mali Lošinj on the latter is connected by ferry to Zadar and by catamaran to Zadar and Pula (both www.jadrolinija. hr). There's also a small (passenger-only) ferry between Mali Lošinj and the small islands of Unije (Walk 12),

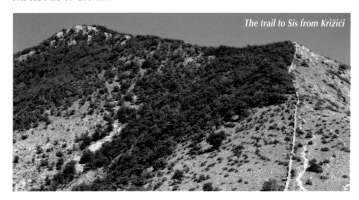

The trail to Sis from Križići

Susak and Ilovik (www.jadrolinija.hr), and the catamaran to Pula also calls at these same islands.

The islands of Cres and Lošinj effectively share the same bus service – there's a regular bus service between Cres town, Osor (Walk 10) and Mali Lošinj (Walk 11). North from Cres town this same service divides into two routes (sometimes passengers have to swap buses in Cres town), one service going via Križići (Walk 8) to Porozina, from where buses continue on the car ferry to Brestova and on to Rijeka and other cities, another going to Merag and crossing on the ferry to the island of Krk, and continuing on to the mainland via the Krk bridge. There are also twice daily buses running between Cres town and Beli (Walk 9), and from Cres town to Lubenice.

Private accommodation in Cres town can be booked through Autotrans (www.autotrans-turizam.com), which has an office just a few metres downhill from the bus station in Cres town. In Beli there's the excellent Pansion Tramuntana (www.beli-tramontana. com).

MAPS

SMAND Otok Cres (sheet 21a, 1:25,000/1:75,000); Otok Cres – Tramuntana: eco trails and labyrinths, available free from the tourist information office in Cres town.

OTHER ESSENTIALS

There are ATMs, supermarkets and pharmacies in Cres old town, and an excellent little spaghetteria/trattoria in the backstreets of Cres town, Al Buon Gusto (Sv Sidar 14; tel. +385 (0)51 571 878) – well worth seeking out in favour of the overpriced places along the waterfront.

WALK 8

Sis

Start/Finish	Križići (380m)
Distance	2.5km
Time	1hr 10mins
Terrain	Steep rocky path, but no technical difficulties
Highest point	Sis (639m)
Maps	SMAND Otok Cres (sheet 21a, 1:25,000/1:75,000). Otok Cres – Tramuntana
Access	Regular bus service between Mali Lošinj (on Lošinj), Cres town and Porozina. Ask to be dropped at Križići, roughly halfway between Cres and Porozina, where road branches off to Beli. Bus picks up here too (see bus timetables for departure times from Porozina; buses arrive at Križići from Porozina around 15mins later). Twice daily bus service between Cres and Beli also stops at Križići (arrives at Križići around 10mins after listed departure times from Beli).

A short, steep route to Sis – usually described as the highest point on Cres, despite Gorice, a little further along the ridge, actually being slightly higher at 648m – with excellent views.

From **Križići**, at the corner between the main road and the road to Beli, follow the trail markings alongside the concrete wind barrier and then head steeply uphill on a path with a drystone wall on the left. Turn around occasionally for views of Krk and (on the mainland beyond) the arc of the Gorski Kotar and Velika Kapela mountains, as well as Rijeka; also keep an eye out for griffon

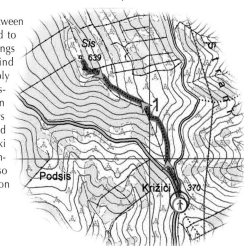

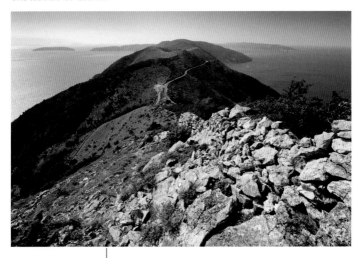

Looking south to Križići and beyond from the trail to Sis

vultures. About 40mins from Križići, arrive on the rocky summit of **Sis** (638m).

The **view** from Sis stretches back along the spine of Cres to Cres Bay (although Cres town itself is not visible), with Valun on the far side, Helm above this and Osorščica (Walk 10) on the island of Lošinj beyond. To the west the Istrian coast is visible, from the towering red-and-white striped chimney at Plomin to Premantura, the long indented cape at the southern tip of the Istrian peninsula.

Descend to **Križići** by the same route (allow 30mins).

WALK 9
Tramuntana

Start/Finish	Pansion Tramuntana, Beli (150m)
Distance	7km
Time	3hrs 20mins
Terrain	Easy walk, with short section on 4WD track then forest paths and tracks (rocky at times); route finding quite difficult in places
Highest point	325m
Maps	SMAND Otok Cres (sheet 21a, 1:25,000/1:75,000). Otok Cres – Tramuntana (**note** although this covers all the marked trails around Beli in reasonable detail, the thick colours/labels marking each route obscure the surrounding terrain/landmarks and make it very difficult to use)
Access	Twice daily bus between Cres and Beli – walkers must catch early morning bus from Cres (and it is very early!) and return late afternoon. More regular bus service between Cres town and Porozina drops off and picks up from Križići (start of Walk 8), where road branches off to Beli. From there it's about 7km road walk to Beli. Avoid all this by staying in Beli.

A walk very unlike most in this guide, as it goes through thick woodland on a maze of old forest trails, passing abandoned hamlets and several landscape art labyrinths.

Turn right outside Pansion Tramuntana in **Beli** and walk uphill, then follow the road around to the right. Pass a wooden cross on the left and a small concrete sculpture on the right, ignoring a road on the left. Some 20mins from Pansion Tramuntana turn left following the red/purple trail markings, turn right through a wall and go along a forest path to reach a moss-covered ruined stone house. Go right on a walled path, then left over a broken wall. Go downhill passing an area of subsidence on the right to arrive at the Ishtar maze (**L3** on the route map), 1hr from Beli.

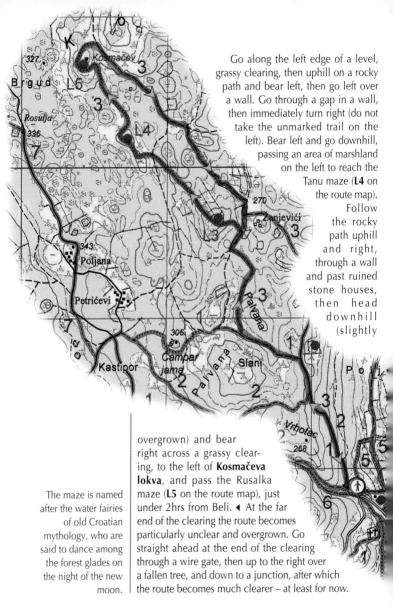

Go along the left edge of a level, grassy clearing, then uphill on a rocky path and bear left, then go left over a wall. Go through a gap in a wall, then immediately turn right (do not take the unmarked trail on the left). Bear left and go downhill, passing an area of marshland on the left to reach the Tanu maze (**L4** on the route map). Follow the rocky path uphill and right, through a wall and past ruined stone houses, then head downhill (slightly overgrown) and bear right across a grassy clearing, to the left of **Kosmačeva lokva**, and pass the Rusalka maze (**L5** on the route map), just under 2hrs from Beli. ◄ At the far end of the clearing the route becomes particularly unclear and overgrown. Go straight ahead at the end of the clearing through a wire gate, then up to the right over a fallen tree, and down to a junction, after which the route becomes much clearer – at least for now.

The maze is named after the water fairies of old Croatian mythology, who are said to dance among the forest glades on the night of the new moon.

The abandoned village of Žanjevići in Tramuntana

Turn right (marked 'Beli') on a broad, walled trail, passing tracks on the left until the ruined village of **Žanjevići** is reached, a short distance up a path on the left. ▶ Return to the main trail and turn left, rejoining the outgoing route and following this back to the road and Pansion Tramuntana in **Beli**.

This is one of many villages in the area to have been abandoned during the 20th century as people moved to towns.

OTHER WALKS ON CRES

Lubenice
The path from the spectacular cliff-top village of Lubenice down to the beach of Sv Ivan below descends some 380m and takes around 45mins (allow at least 1hr to walk back up).

anjska

Sv Salvadur and Sv Blaž
A signposted walled track can be followed northwest from Cres town (starting from near the cemetery, at the far end of Zagrebačka ulica and S Gavza) to the 19th-century church of Sv Salvadur, and then further along a rocky path to Sv Blaž, a small rocky cove popular with boat excursions from Cres town (which unfortunately can lead to a surprising amount of litter for such a remote spot).

U.Vrtac

LOŠINJ

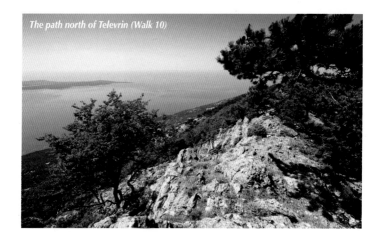

The path north of Televrin (Walk 10)

Divided from Cres only by a narrow artificial channel spanned by a road bridge, Lošinj continues the general north–south orientation of its larger neighbour, surrounded by a scattering of smaller islands and islets (Unije, Susak, Ilovik and Vele and Male Srakane). The northern half of the island is dominated by the long ridge of Osoršćica (Walk 10), including the highest point of the island, Televrin (588m).

The main town, Mali Lošinj, sits at the head of a long natural inlet on the island's west coast. The nearby town of Veli Lošinj (Walk 11) on the east coast is actually the smaller of the island's two eponymous settlements, which may cause some confusion as mali means 'small' and veli means 'large'. Veli Lošinj was originally the larger of the two, but Mali Lošinj grew in size and importance under Austrian rule during the 19th century as a centre for shipbuilding and as a popular holiday spot for the well-heeled Austrian elite around the end of the 19th century. Their elegant villas are still visible at Čikat, the lush pine-forested area just west of Mali Lošinj.

Lošinj was also the site of one of Croatia's most sensational archaeological finds, the discovery in 1997 of the so-called Croatian Apoxyomenos – an intact life-sized bronze Roman statue dating from the first century BC or the first century AD. Copied from

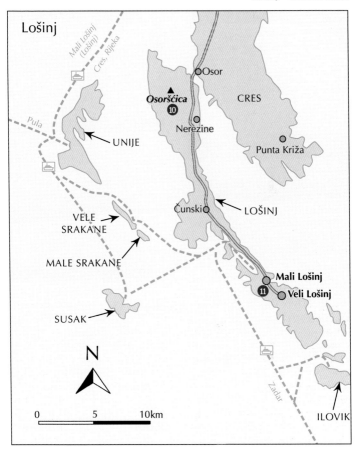

Lošinj

Mali Lošinj (Lošinj)
Cres, Rijeka
Osor
Osoršćica 10
CRES
Pula
Nerezine
UNIJE
Punta Križa
Čunski
LOŠINJ
VELE SRAKANE
MALE SRAKANE
Mali Lošinj
11 Veli Lošinj
SUSAK
N
0   5   10km
Zadar
ILOVIK

a fourth-century BC Greek original, it was found by chance in the waters off the nearby islet of Vela Orjula, just off the southeast coast of Lošinj.

Dolphins are often sighted off the shores of Lošinj, and have been monitored and researched for several years by the Blue World Institute of Marine Research and Conservation (www.blue-world.org), which is based in Veli Lošinj.

105

THE ISLANDS OF CROATIA

TOURIST INFORMATION

The tourist information office in Mali Lošinj is on the waterfront, between where the ferry/catamaran moors and the head of the harbour (Riva lošinjskih kapetana 29; tel. +385 (0)51 231 884; www.tz-malilosinj.hr).

GETTING THERE AND GETTING AROUND

Mali Lošinj is connected by ferry to Zadar and by catamaran to Zadar and Pula (both www.jadrolinija.hr). Another catamaran (www.krilo.hr) sails between Mali Lošinj, Cres and Rijeka. There's also a small (passenger-only) ferry between Mali Lošinj and the small islands of Unije (Walk 12), Susak and Ilovik (www.jadrolinija.hr), and the catamaran to Pula also calls at these same islands.

There's a good local bus service between Mali Lošinj and the island of Cres, starting in Veli Lošinj and stopping at Mali Lošinj, Nerezine (Walk 10), Osor (Walk 10) and Cres, before continuing by one of two routes to Rijeka or Zagreb on the mainland, either via the ferry from Merag to Valbiska on the island of Krk, and from there over the bridge to the mainland, or via Križići (Walk 8) and the ferry from Porozina to the mainland. There's

also a frequent shuttle bus between Mali Lošinj and the hotels at Čikat and Sunčana uvala. The bus station in Mali Lošinj is at one end of the waterfront, just across the road from where the ferry from Zadar docks.

ACCOMMODATION

The nicest place to stay in Mali Lošinj is Hotel Aurora (www.losinj-hotels. com) out by Sunčana uvala (the buffet meals are excellent, so it's well worth getting half-board). Private accommodation can be booked through ASL Agency, in Veli Lošinj (www. island-losinj.com).

MAPS

Lošinj – Tourist and Trekking Map (HGSS; 1:25,000) is available from the tourist information office in Mali Lošinj. 'Lošinj promenades and footpaths', available free from the tourist information office, is also useful as it lists the timings of different sections of various walks on the island.

OTHER ESSENTIALS

There are ATMs, supermarkets and pharmacies in the old town. Bikes can be rented through ASL (see above).

WALK 10
Osorščica

Start	Nerezine bus stop (25m)
Finish	Osor (on Cres) (2m)
Distance	12km
Time	4hrs 45mins
Terrain	Clear but rocky path, with some boulder-hopping between Počivalice and Sv Mikul; short section on asphalt at beginning and 4WD track at end
Highest point	Televrin (588m)
Maps	Lošinj – Tourist and Trekking Map (HGSS, 1:25,000). Less detailed 'Lošinj promenades and footpaths'. Sv Mikul (both peak and church) is sometimes written 'Sv Nikola', including on the 'Promenades and footpaths' map.
Access	Regular bus service between Mali Lošinj and Cres town (on Cres) stops at Nerezine and Osor. Bus timetables list departure times from Cres town; expect buses to arrive at Osor from Cres around 40mins later. For those staying in Nerezine, it's possible to walk back there from Osor on a path that runs along the waterfront for part of the way.

This outstanding walk is one of the better-known routes on the islands. It leads over the long, spectacularly rocky spine of Osorščica in the north of the island, taking in Televrin, the highest point on Lošinj, to finish at Osor, just over the narrow channel on the island of Cres. A trail to Televrin was marked as early as the 1880s, when members of a local tourist association led the Austrian Crown Prince Rudolf to the summit.

▶ From the bus stop at **Nerezine**, turn left (towards Mali Lošinj) and follow the slip road uphill, ignoring a track on the right signposted to Sv Mikul and Televrin (a more direct, although inferior route). Just after a sharp bend in the road turn right up a lane marked 'Osorščica, Sv Mikul, Počivalice and Tomožina', passing a small café. Turn left onto a marked footpath, a little overgrown in places, then go under the main road through a low-ceilinged concrete underpass.

The bus stop at Nerezine is just above the town on a slip road which branches off the main Mali Lošinj–Cres road near Sv Jakov.

On the far side, turn right very briefly along a drainage channel then left up a good rocky path, bearing left and contouring the hillside, with good views of the Velebit mountains running along the coast on the mainland. Pass a trail to Tomožina and Čunski on the

map continues on page 110

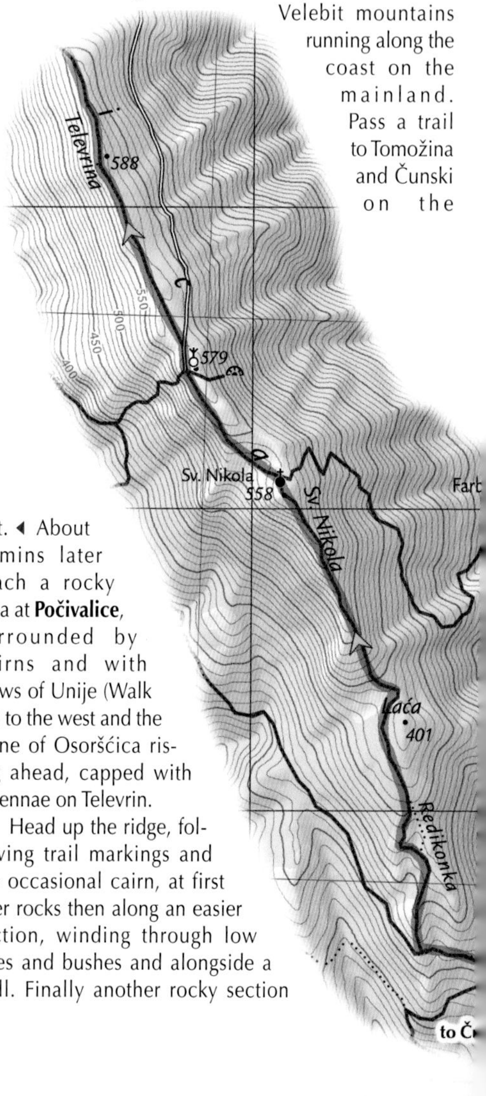

left. ◄ About 15mins later reach a rocky area at **Počivalice**, surrounded by cairns and with views of Unije (Walk 12) to the west and the spine of Osoršćica rising ahead, capped with antennae on Televrin.

Head up the ridge, following trail markings and the occasional cairn, at first over rocks then along an easier section, winding through low trees and bushes and alongside a wall. Finally another rocky section

Tomožina, on the west coast, can be reached in around 1hr. The trail to Čunski leads almost all the way to Mali Lošinj, joining the main road near Čunski almost 4hrs away, and passing Polanža, the site of a Bronze Age fort (see 'Other walks on Lošinj and Susak'; page 117).

Televrina •588

•579

Sv. Nikola 558

Sv. Nikola

Fart

Lača •401

Redikonka

to Č

with spectacular views back along the entire length of the island leads to the small church of Sv Mikul (**Sv Nikola** on the route map;

The trail on Osoršćica, looking south

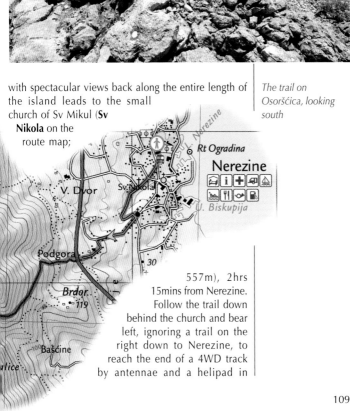

557m), 2hrs 15mins from Nerezine. Follow the trail down behind the church and bear left, ignoring a trail on the right down to Nerezine, to reach the end of a 4WD track by antennae and a helipad in

According to legend, Sv Gaudencije (St Gaudentius), Bishop of Osor in the 11th century, lived in this cave for a period of time, when he is credited with banishing snakes from the island.

15mins. From here a trail on the right leads to Jama Sv Gaudencije. ◄ Another trail on the left leads down by a steep trail with fixed cables and ropes to Vela jama (a cave inhabited during the Middle Palaeolithic Era). Go straight ahead on the 4WD track, then turn left onto a marked footpath. The path goes at first through woodland then over more open, rocky ground, to reach **Televrin** (588m), the highest point on Osoršćica, 15mins from the trail to Vela jama.

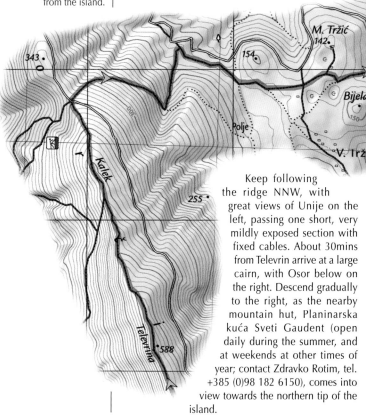

Keep following the ridge NNW, with great views of Unije on the left, passing one short, very mildly exposed section with fixed cables. About 30mins from Televrin arrive at a large cairn, with Osor below on the right. Descend gradually to the right, as the nearby mountain hut, Planinarska kuća Sveti Gaudent (open daily during the summer, and at weekends at other times of year; contact Zdravko Rotim, tel. +385 (0)98 182 6150), comes into view towards the northern tip of the island.

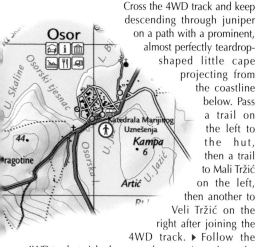

Cross the 4WD track and keep descending through juniper on a path with a prominent, almost perfectly teardrop-shaped little cape projecting from the coastline below. Pass a trail on the left to the hut, then a trail to Mali Tržić on the left, then another to Veli Tržić on the right after joining the 4WD track. ▶ Follow the 4WD track straight down past the campsite and over the bridge into **Osor**, on the island of Cres, 2hrs from Televrin.

Mali and Veli Tržić are two small abandoned hamlets, where Sv Gaudencije (St Gaudentius) is thought to have been born, and can be reached in 5mins and 20mins respectively.

Osor was the island's capital until the 15th century, in control of the narrow channel between the two islands (and therefore shipping in this part of the

On the descent towards Osor (on Cres) from Televrin

111

Adriatic, until the advent of steam), and still has several grand buildings to show for it, despite its dwindling population.

The bus stop in Osor is just along the road from the bridge (on the Cres side), near some cafés.

The **bridge** between Cres and Lošinj opens (meaning pedestrians and traffic can't cross between the two islands) to let boats through twice a day, at around 09.00 and again at 17.00, for about 30mins each time. It is advisable to be on the far (Osor/Cres) side of the bridge before it opens and to wait for the bus there (there are no cafés on the Lošinj side of the bridge, and the bus is unlikely, after waiting on the Cres side for the road to reopen, to stop on the Lošinj side of the bridge).

WALK 11
Veli Lošinj – The Dolphin Way

Start/Finish	Mali Lošinj (2m)
Distance	9.5km
Time	3hrs 50mins
Terrain	Easy coastal path, followed by a broad rocky track up to Sv Ivan, a short section on asphalt in Mali Lošinj and again in Veli Lošinj, then a concrete seaside promenade from the latter
Highest point	Sv Ivan (231m)
Maps	Lošinj – Tourist and Trekking Map (HGSS, 1:25,000). Less detailed 'Lošinj promenades and footpaths'. Sunčana uvala is marked as 'Sunčina u.' on the route map.
Access	*Optional start at Sunčana uvala*: frequent bus service from Mali Lošinj to hotels at Čikat and Sunčana uvala – get off at last stop, by Hotel Aurora, and walk down to waterfront (past main hotel entrance then right beside swimming pools). *Optional finish at Veli Lošinj*: regular bus service links Veli and Mali Lošinj with Cres town (on Cres).

This short, easy walk includes a stretch of coast from Sunčana uvala, passing several nice beaches and secluded coves, before it arrives at Veli Lošinj, then heads back to Mali Lošinj along a pleasant seaside promenade. There are plenty of opportunities to stop for a dip. Dolphins are a not uncommon sight in the waters around Lošinj, and this walk is sometimes called The Dolphin Way.

Start from the far end of the square (Trg Republike Hrvatske) at the head of the harbour in Mali Lošinj and walk up an alley following the signs to DM (chemist/supermarket), then after passing DM walk up the steps to the main road. Cross the main road and follow the road opposite towards Hotel Aurora (there's a walled path beside the road), then before reaching the Aurora take a path on the right down to the waterfront and beach at Sunčana uvala, 25mins from Mali Lošinj. ▶

Alternatively, start at Sunčana uvala to shorten the walk by 25mins.

Turn left and follow the waterfront SE below Hotel Aurora, walking along a concrete path above rocky swimming spots. After the bar at Borik follow a marked

The island of Susak, seen at sunset from the waterfront near Sunčana uvala

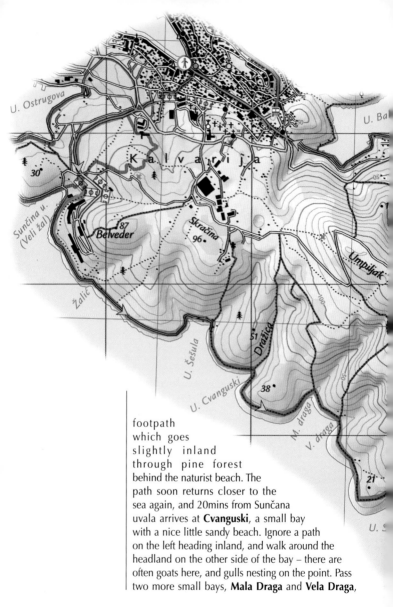

U. Ostrugova

U. Ba

Kalvarija

30°

Suncína u.
(Veli žal)

87
Belveder

Skračina
96

Žalić

Umpiljak

U. Šešula

Dražica

51

U. Cvanguski

38

M. draga

V. draga

21

U. S

footpath
which goes
slightly inland
through pine forest
behind the naturist beach. The
path soon returns closer to the
sea again, and 20mins from Sunčana
uvala arrives at **Cvanguski**, a small bay
with a nice little sandy beach. Ignore a path
on the left heading inland, and walk around the
headland on the other side of the bay – there are
often goats here, and gulls nesting on the point. Pass
two more small bays, **Mala Draga** and **Vela Draga**,

again ignoring trails leading inland, then cut across the
headland after Vela Draga to reach **Sunfarni**, a larger
bay 90mins from Sunčana uvala. Cut across the next
headland to arrive at **Krivica**, a deep, sheltered
inlet which is a popular mooring spot for
yachts, in 15mins.

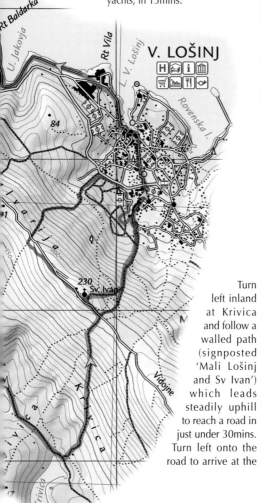

Turn
left inland
at Krivica
and follow a
walled path
(signposted
'Mali Lošinj
and Sv Ivan')
which leads
steadily uphill
to reach a road in
just under 30mins.
Turn left onto the
road to arrive at the

small church of **Sv Ivan** (St John) on the right, built in 1755 as a votive chapel for the local Sforzina family.

Follow the path downhill towards Veli Lošinj from just below the church, passing a series of large wooden crosses and a small devotional shrine. ◀ Pass a marked trail on the left which goes through a wall and down to the car park, and keep straight ahead below tall stone walls (which appear a little unstable at one point). Turn left onto a stone paved track between houses with faint trail markings, cross the main road and keep going down past the church to arrive at the cluster of cafés and restaurants on the waterfront of the pretty little harbour at **Veli Lošinj**, 35mins from Sv Ivan.

This path is a Via crusis (Way of the Cross) between Veli Lošinj and Sv Ivan.

Veli Lošinj, as its name implies (*veli* means 'big'), was once the largest settlement on the island, before Mali Lošinj (*mali* means 'small') grew to its present size during the shipbuilding boom of the 19th century under Austria–Hungary. The Blue World Institute of Marine Research and Conservation (www.blue-world.org), based in Veli Lošinj, has been monitoring and researching dolphins in the waters around Cres, Lošinj and Vis

The harbour at Veli Lošinj

for several years. It was the first marine education centre to open on the eastern Adriatic coast, and the Centre helped establish the Cres–Lošinj Marine Protected Area, the first such area for dolphins in the entire Mediterranean.

Walk left around the waterfront (passing the Blue World Marine Education Centre on the left) and follow the road up, then down, past hotels to reach a pleasant seaside promenade which follows the coast back towards Mali Lošinj. After 35mins, at the head of the first inlet of the second bay, follow a broad concrete track inland (marked 'centar') to reach the main road and bus route. Go more or less straight ahead over this and down to the main square (Trg Republike Hrvatske) on the waterfront in **Mali Lošinj**. ▸

To return to the hotels at Čikat and Sunčana uvala, take a bus or follow the route as described at the start of the walk – it's more pleasant than following the main road.

OTHER WALKS ON LOŠINJ AND SUSAK

Čunski to Počivalica
It's possible to follow a longer route over Osoršćica than the one described in Walk 10, starting from Čunski on the main road just north of Mali Lošinj and climbing initially to Polanža (site of a Bronze Age fort), then continuing on a path all the way to Počivalica, on Walk 10. To get to Čunski take the Mali Lošinj–Cres bus and get off at, or just after, the road on the left to the small airstrip; the trail starts a short distance after this on the left. The route is less popular than the shorter route from Nerezine (Walk 10), so the path may be a little more overgrown.

Susak
Like Unije further north (Walk 12), the small island of Susak, off the west coast of Lošinj, makes an interesting day out from Mali Lošinj. There's a footpath to Vela Straža, at a grand total of 91m the highest point on the island, as well as to Arat, the headland to the east of Susak village. For ferry connections see the introduction to Unije; page 119.

UNIJE

The Jadrolinija ferry 'Premuda', departing from Unije

The largest and the furthest west of the scattering of islands off the coast of Lošinj, Unije is a quiet little place with a population of only 88. The island was inhabited at least as early as the Bronze Age, and the remains of a Roman villa have been found, along with a Roman road linking Maračol and Podkujni bays.

Unije is unusual for the thick layer of loess and sand deposits which covers part of the island – a distinction it shares with the neighbouring islands of Susak, Vele and Male Srakane. The deposits, which on Unije cover the island's flat western peninsula, Unijsko polje (Walk 12), are thought to originate from the River Po in Italy, and to have been laid down during the last Ice Age.

The fertile peninsula of Unijsko polje (*polje* simply means 'fields' in Croatian) has been prized for centuries – although notably the land and its lucrative crops (particularly grapes) never belonged to the local inhabitants, but to wealthy landowners in Osor on the island of Cres during the medieval period, and later to wealthy families on Lošinj. The local population of Unije simply worked the land and harvested the crops for the landowners, growing their own crops in karst depressions in the north of the island, until the land of Unijsko polje was sold to them in the early part of the 20th century.

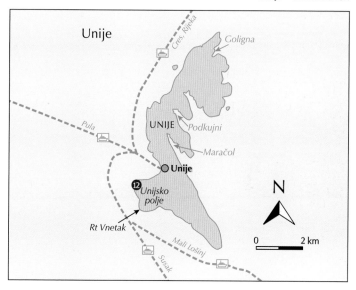

TOURIST INFORMATION

The tourist information office in Mali Lošinj is on the waterfront, between where the ferry/catamaran moors and the head of the harbour (Riva lošinjskih kapetana 29; tel. +385 (0)51 231 884; www.tz-malilosinj.hr). The website www.unije.de also has useful information on the island, as do www.otok-unije.com (Croatian only) and www.unije.si.

GETTING THERE AND GETTING AROUND

A small (passenger-only) ferry, the *Premuda*, sails twice daily between Mali Lošinj and Unije, Susak and Ilovik, running supplies to the islands

(www.jadrolinija.hr). Out of season the *Premuda* doesn't call at Unije on Wednesdays, and calls only once on Mondays. The first sailing from Mali Lošinj is very early (05.00), but as consolation this means you'll arrive at Unije just as the sun breaks over the spine of the island. If it's rough weather, expect the open outside seats on the lower deck to get suitably drenched – in which case take refuge in the small bar or on the open upper deck. The catamaran between Zadar and Pula (www.jadrolinija.hr) also calls at Unije, Susak and Ilovik before or after stopping at Mali Lošinj, but doesn't call at Unije every day (Monday, Friday and Sunday in the summer; Wednesday and Saturday

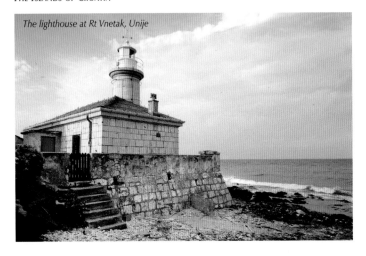

The lighthouse at Rt Vnetak, Unije

out of season). Another catamaran, which sails between Mali Lošinj, Cres and Rijeka (www.krilo.hr), also calls at Unije five times a week. The catamaran departs from the same spot as the Zadar ferry in Mali Lošinj; the *Premuda* docks about halfway back along the waterfront towards the town centre.

There are no cars or other road transport on Unije.

ACCOMMODATION

This walk can easily be done as a day trip from Mali Lošinj, where accommodation is plentiful (see the introduction to Lošinj; page 106), providing you get the early ferry. If you want to stay on Unije, try Pansion Unijana (www.unijana.hr).

MAPS

Lošinj – Tourist and Trekking map (HGSS, 1:25,000). 'Lošinj promenades and footpaths' and 'Otok Unije – attractions' are both available free from the tourist information office in Mali Lošinj, although neither is particularly detailed.

OTHER ESSENTIALS

There are just a small handful of restaurants, cafés and grocery shops in Unije, so bring whatever you need with you.

WALK 12
Rt Vnetak

Start/Finish	Jetty where the ferry/catamaran departs in Unije village (2m)
Distance	5.5km
Time	1hr 15mins
Terrain	Rocky or pebbly beach, then up a loess bank and back on a level grassy track
Highest point	<5m
Maps	'Lošinj promenades and footpaths' or 'Otok Unije – attractions'. **Note** The former incorrectly places the lighthouse on the northern point of the peninsula, Rt Nart, instead of on Rt Vnetak. Lošinj – Tourist and Trekking map (HGSS, 1:25,000) also covers Unije in more detail.
Access	There are no cars or buses on Unije, so it's a simply case of arrive by ferry, then walk.

A short, very easy walk around Unijsko polje, the fertile peninsula to the southwest of Unije, to the 19th-century lighthouse at Rt Vnetak. The route around the headland is on the beach itself, which is narrow and backed by steep loess banks, so it shouldn't be attempted in poor weather or if the sea is rough.

From the small ferry ticket office on the pier in **Unije** village, turn right along the waterfront and keep following the shoreline around the bay, initially on a path above the beach. Then continue along the beach itself, over pebbles and dried seaweed, with sheep and Istrian cattle peering out over the banks on the left. Walk around the first headland, **Rt Nart** (caution – the rocks can be slippery), with a tall bank of loess topped with reeds on the left. ▶ About 50mins from the ferry ticket office, arrive at the next headland, **Rt Vnetak**, with its lighthouse.

The soft loess, laid down during the last Ice Age, is one of the things which makes Unije and neighbouring Susak unique among Croatia's Adriatic islands.

The **lighthouse** dates from 1873, and from alongside it there are good views of Susak and the southern

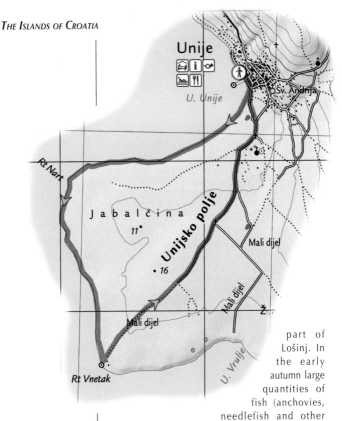

part of Lošinj. In the early autumn large quantities of fish (anchovies, needlefish and other pelagic species) can be found in the seas off Rt Vnetak – perhaps another reason for early settlement on the island – and according to one story the foreman involved in building the lighthouse was dragged out to sea by an enormous tuna, never to be seen again.

In August 2013 the area was populated with an extraordinary number of small blue butterflies.

Scramble up the steep loess bank just before the lighthouse, then follow a clear, easy grassy path across the centre of the fertile Unijsko polje, prized for its crop growing for centuries. ◄ Pass a shrine on the right, go through a gate, then continue straight ahead on a

concrete path, with another shrine on the right and a memorial to the Croatian War of Independence inscribed in the concrete. Bear left to arrive back at the ferry ticket office and pier in **Unije**, 25mins from the lighthouse.

Loess banks on the coast of Unije, along the edge of Unijsko polje

OTHER WALKS ON UNIJE

Maračol to Goligna

For a longer walk on the island, walk from Unije village to Maračol Bay, and from there up to Goligna, near the northern tip of the island. The route follows an old Roman road for part of the way.

PAG

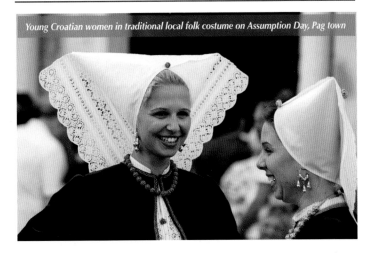

Young Croatian women in traditional local folk costume on Assumption Day, Pag town

The long, slender island of Pag is separated from the mainland and the Velebit mountains by the narrow Velebitski kanal (Velebit channel), and is linked to the mainland by a road bridge, Pag bridge (Paški most), in the south. There is very little in the way of trees and maquis on Pag, the island having lost most of its former woodland to Venetian shipbuilding centuries ago, and on much of the island vegetation is limited to a few hardy aromatic herbs and grasses. The barren moonscape of its Furnaža peninsula gives a particularly harsh impression when viewed from Karlobag on the mainland coast and from the summit of Sv Vid (Walks 13 and 14), the highest point on the island. The

spindly, finger-like Lun peninsula, in the north of the island, provides one of the few counterpoints to this, being noted for its olive groves, some of the trees being over 1000 years old.

Historically, the island owes its wealth and importance to the extensive saltpans which stretch southeast from Pag town, worked since the Roman period and the source of much wrangling between Zadar and Rab over the centuries. Pag town itself has a lovely historic core, with a well-proportioned church (Church of the Assumption of the Virgin Mary) and a Bishop's Palace – although in the end it never did become a bishropic, an enhanced status which would not have suited its more

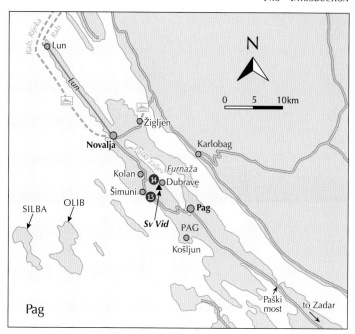

Pag

powerful neighbours Zadar and Rab. The island's most popular beach, Zrče, is near Novalja, towards the north of the island.

Pag is famous for its exquisitely intricate hand-sewn lace (*paška čipka*), which is inscribed on the UNESCO List of Intangible Cultural Heritage. Traditionally, the sewing work is carried out without the use of any formal patterns – instead, designs are passed down over generations between grandmothers, mothers and daughters, becoming embellished and personalized, and effectively making each piece unique. It takes around 24hrs to create a piece the size of a small saucer – anything with a price tag which doesn't reflect that amount of work is probably not the genuine article. Genuine pieces can be bought in the Lace Museum, in the former Bishop's Palace. Pag is also famous for its sheep's cheese (*paški sir*), which is among the best in Croatia. In Pag town on Assumption Day (Velika Gospa) there's a procession in which a statue of the Virgin Mary (Gospe od Staroga Grada) is carried from a shrine to the Church of the Assumption of the Virgin Mary in the town centre.

TOURIST INFORMATION

The tourist information office in Pag town is in the old town between the bridge and the main square (Od Špitala 2; tel. +385 (0)23 611 286; www.tzgpag.hr). The Zadar County Tourist Board also has plenty of useful information (Sv Leopolda B Mandia 1, Zadar; tel. +385 (023) 315 316; www.zadar.hr).

GETTING THERE AND GETTING AROUND

Pag is connected to the mainland by a road bridge (Paški most), and there are regular buses from Zadar to both Pag town and Novalja (www.antoniotours.hr), passing Šimuni, the start of Walk 13. There's a daily (during summer) catamaran service between Novalja, Rab and Rijeka (www.jadrolinija.hr), departing early in the morning from Novalja and arriving back in Novalja late in the evening (in the early part of the summer this will be after the last bus leaves for Pag/Zadar – unfortunately the start dates for summer bus and catamaran timetables are not synchronised). A ferry runs between Žigljen and Prizna on the mainland (www.jadrolinija.hr) – some buses between Zadar and Zagreb travel via Pag, using this ferry route. There's also a small passenger boat (daily during summer, www.rapska-plovidba.hr) between Lun, at the far end of the island's long northwestern peninsula, and the island of Rab, although no public transport between Novalja and Lun (a taxi will cost around 200kn).

ACCOMMODATION

Private accommodation in Pag town can be booked through Mediteran (www.mediteranpag.com), which has an office just around the corner from the bus station. Nena Brban's apartments (tel. +385 (0)23 600 252, +385 (0)95 5988 599) are recommended, a 10min walk west of the old town.

MAPS

Island Pag Trekking and Mountain Biking is available free from the tourist information office in Pag town, although the scale of this is really too small for hiking purposes, and the map is more geared towards cyclists.

OTHER ESSENTIALS

There are ATMs, supermarkets and pharmacies in both Pag town and Novalja. The bus station in Pag town (for buses to Novalja or Zadar) is a 5min walk north from the old town bridge along the waterfront, near Mediteran. The bus station in Novalja is a 15min walk from the catamaran (turn right from the bus station, then right onto the main road and keep straight ahead to the waterfront, where the catamaran departure point is on your right); otherwise a minibus runs between the bus station and the catamaran.

WALK 13
Šimuni to Sv Vid

Start/Finish	Main Pag–Novalja road, opposite entrance to Camp Šimuni (35m)
Distance	6.5km
Time	2hrs 30mins
Terrain	Clear, rocky path over easy, quite gentle slopes
Highest point	Sv Vid (348m) (marked as 349m on recommended map)
Maps	Island Pag Trekking and Mountain Biking
Access	Regular bus service between towns of Pag and Novalja – ask to be dropped at entrance to Camp Šimuni (directly opposite start of walk). On return, make yourself visible when waiting for bus. *Heading to Pag town*: bus arrives at Camp Šimuni around 15mins after listed departure times from Novalja; *heading for Novalja*: bus arrives around 10mins after listed departure times from Pag.

An easy, well-marked route to the summit of Sv Vid, the highest point on the island of Pag, across the gentle western slopes of this mountain. The walk is at its best when combined with Walk 14 – the steep eastern slopes of Sv Vid on that route providing a good contrast to the route described here. The light on Sv Vid just before dusk can be spectacular, turning the western slopes (and those of the Velebit range on the mainland) an almost lurid orange or crimson – but take a torch for the return journey if you're returning late.

Note that there's no shade on this route, and Pag can be relentlessly hot during the summer. Try to complete this route in the morning or leave it for the late afternoon, and thereby avoid walking in the middle of the day.

From the **main road** opposite the entrance to Camp Šimuni, follow the trail markings and turn inland on the short asphalted road marked 'Sveti Vid, Dubrave and Kolan'. Go straight ahead at the end of the asphalt road onto a 4WD track, head through a gate and then go right onto a clear path, with the small church on the summit of Sv Vid clearly visible ahead.

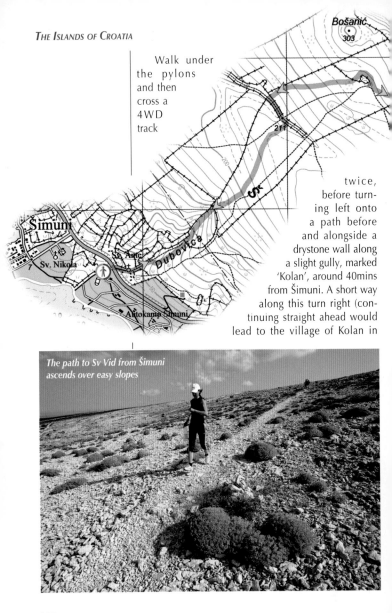

Walk under the pylons and then cross a 4WD track twice, before turning left onto a path before and alongside a drystone wall along a slight gully, marked 'Kolan', around 40mins from Šimuni. A short way along this turn right (continuing straight ahead would lead to the village of Kolan in

The path to Sv Vid from Šimuni ascends over easy slopes

around 30mins), following trail markings and cairns and bearing ENE towards the church. ▶ Pass a small pond on the right, then ascend to the crest of the ridge and the small church on the summit of **Sv Vid** (348m), 90mins from Šimuni.

Note the drystone walls on the hillside in the shape of an enormous crucifix.

The **views** on reaching the crest of the ridge are breathtaking. The Velebit mountains run in a wall along the coast of the mainland to the northeast, viewed across the Pag Inlet (Paški zaljev) and the desiccated moonscape of the Furnaža peninsula. Pag town is clearly visible to the southeast, and beyond it the expanse of salt pans which have provided the island with a source of wealth since Antiquity. The island of Ugljan lies to the south, with its two prominent hills (the one on the right is Šćah, Walk 15), and to the southwest is the island of Dugi otok (the high area towards the right is Orljak, Walk 16). The small church of Sv Vid, now in ruins, dates from the 14th century.

The summit of Sv Vid

Descend to **Šimuni** by the same route (allow 1hr), or follow one of the alternatives below.

Continuation to Dubrave
A recommended alternative is to follow Walk 14 in reverse, descending over the steep, and at times slightly exposed, trail to Dubrave. Note that there's no public transport from Dubrave (it's a 1hr road walk from Dubrave back to Pag town).

Alternative return route
Another option is to retrace your steps as far as the junction with the trail to Kolan, and turn right onto this to reach the main Pag–Novalja road near the village of Kolan in 30mins. Here it is possible to flag down a bus (although it may be harder for buses to stop here than at Šimuni).

WALK 14
Dubrave to Sv Vid

Start/Finish	Dubrave (45m)
Distance	2km
Time	2hrs (signs on this route give timings between Dubrave and Sv Vid as 45mins up and 30mins down – perhaps a little optimistic)
Terrain	Steep, rocky and slightly exposed in places, with some sections over scree. **Note** Do not attempt if the bura is blowing, as there is no shelter from its gale-force gusts.
Highest point	Sv Vid (348m) (marked as 349m on recommended map)
Maps	Island Pag Trekking and Mountain Biking
Access	No public transport to Dubrave, so go by car/taxi or walk from Pag town (1hr each way); there's nowhere secure to leave bikes at bottom of route. For those combining this route with Walk 13 (start/finish Camp Šimuni), regular bus service between Pag and Novalja will drop off or pick up at entrance to Camp Šimuni. There's no obvious settlement to mark Dubrave, but start of trail to Sv Vid is clearly marked (on the left shortly after passing through Sv Marija if coming from Pag).

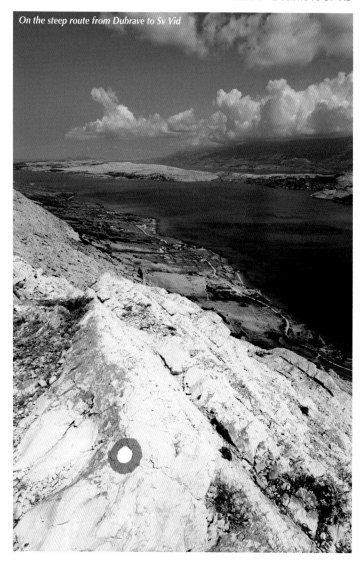

On the steep route from Dubrave to Sv Vid

A much steeper route to the highest point on Pag, Sv Vid, than its counterpart from the west, Walk 13. It is not technically difficult, but steep and rocky with some scree, and a little exposed in places. There are good trail markings and staggeringly good views from the summit. This walk can be combined with Walk 13 to finish at Camp Šimuni, which is easily accessible by public transport, unlike Dubrave. These eastern slopes catch the full force of the sun from fairly early in the morning, but are in shade during the late afternoon and early evening.

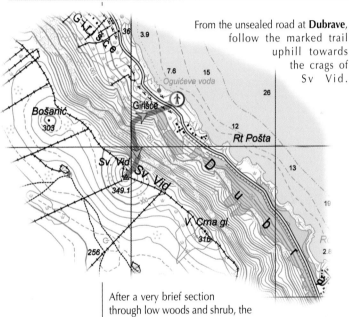

From the unsealed road at **Dubrave**, follow the marked trail uphill towards the crags of Sv Vid.

After a very brief section through low woods and shrub, the trail snakes steeply up over scree, passing twisted outcrops of limestone. It then bears left over rock shelves with some slightly exposed sections to reach the summit of **Sv Vid** (348m) in 1hr. See Walk 13 for a description of the view from the summit.

Return to **Dubrave** by the same route, or continue to Šimuni following the description for Walk 13 in reverse.

UGLJAN

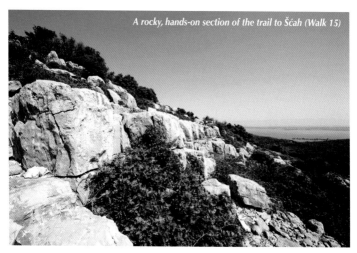
A rocky, hands-on section of the trail to Šćah (Walk 15)

Less than 4km as the crow flies (and just a 25min ferry ride) from Zadar, Ugljan forms the innermost island of the Zadar archipelago – a loose scattering of islands of vastly different sizes which also includes Molat, Ist, Olib and Silba further north, as well as the neighbouring island of Pašman and, further west, the larger Dugi otok (Walks 16–18). Despite its proximity to Zadar (of which it's often described as a suburb) Ugljan feels remarkably green and peaceful, an impression further enhanced by its extensive olive groves – there are over 200,000 olive trees on the island. Long and narrow, Ugljan is separated from Pašman by a narrow channel, dug in the 19th century – the two were formerly a single island, and they are now linked by a road bridge.

The double hump of Ugljan's two main hills, Šćah (286m, Walk 15) and Sv Mihovil (250m), forms a distinctive skyline whether the island is viewed from Zadar or Dugi otok. Of the two it is Sv Mihovil, capped with a ruined fort and bristling with radio antennae, which is by far the most visited. This is a pity, since the route to Šćah is much nicer (following a rocky path, rather than an asphalt road), and the summit is uncluttered by antennae. There's a climbing area on the far, west side of Sv Mihovil.

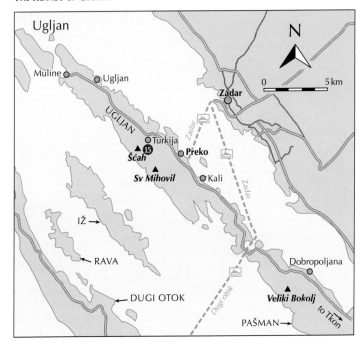

The Liburnians had a fort on Čelinjak, at the northern end of the island. Among the Roman colonists of the first century AD was one Gellia, who gave his name to the island. For many centuries the land on Ugljan belonged to wealthy families in Zadar, but passed to the islanders themselves during the early 20th century. Along with the main settlement, Preko (which is nevertheless very small), there are a string of relatively quiet, unassuming little fishing villages along the island's east coast. Just off-shore from Preko, on the tiny island of Galevac, there's a 15th-century Franciscan monastery.

TOURIST INFORMATION

The tourist information office in Preko is a 15min walk from the ferry dock – along the waterfront, on the far side of the town (Šimuna Kožičića Benje 17; tel. +385 (0)23 288 011; www.ugljan.hr). The Zadar County Tourist Board also has plenty of useful information (Sv Leopolda B Mandia 1, Zadar; tel. +385 (023) 315 316; www.zadar.hr).

GETTING THERE AND GETTING AROUND

There's a frequent ferry between Zadar and Preko (www.jadrolinija.hr), and a regular bus service from Preko to Ugljan town and Muline (the destination is sometimes marked 'Bolnica', meaning 'hospital', which is in Ugljan town), which will drop off and pick up passengers at the beginning of Walk 15. Ugljan is linked to the neighbouring island of Pašman by a road bridge, and the bus service between Muline and Preko continues to Dobropoljana, Kraj and Tkon on Pašman – for timetables see www.ugljan.hr. There's another ferry route between Zadar and Tkon (www.jadrolinija.hr).

ACCOMMODATION

There's a list of private accommodation on the tourist board website (www.ugljan.hr), or bookings can be made through Nav Travel in Preko (www.navadriatic.com).

MAPS

Island Ugljan Map – Olive's island (approx 1:28,000, with contour lines) is available free from the tourist information office in Preko. The same map covers Pašman, on the reverse, in similar detail. With the exception of the route from Turkija to Šćah (Walk 15), and the road walk to Sv Mihovil (see 'Other walks on Ugljan and Pašman'; page 138), several of the hiking routes marked on this and other maps available from the tourist information office are unfortunately quite overgrown and can be very difficult to follow.

OTHER ESSENTIALS

There is an ATM, supermarkets and a pharmacy in Preko, and at the bakery by the bus station and Jadrolinija office can be found some of the best homemade apple strudel (*domaće štrudle od jabuke*) anywhere in Croatia. Bikes can be rented through Nav Travel www.navadriatic.com.

WALK 15
Šćah

Start/Finish	Bus stop on the main Preko–Ugljan road, at turnoff to Turkija (63m)
Distance	4km
Time	2hrs
Terrain	Short section on asphalt, then a good, clear rocky path, with some boulder-hopping towards the summit
Highest point	Šćah (286m)
Maps	Island Ugljan Map – Olive's island [*sic*]. (The correct translation is 'Olive Island'.)
Access	Regular (roughly hourly) bus service between Preko and Ugljan (bus may be marked 'Bolnica' or 'Muline'). Bus stops and picks up at turnoff to the village of Turkija (say 'Za Turkije') (bus stop/ shelter). Regular and frequent ferry service to Preko from Zadar makes it easy to visit Ugljan as day trip from Zadar.

A short walk to the highest point on Ugljan, the tongue-twisting Šćah (pronounced 'shchah'). It follows a well-marked path with some lovely rocky sections, and is much nicer than the more popular (and less interesting) road walk up Sv Mihovil.

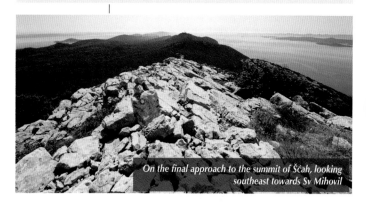

On the final approach to the summit of Šćah, looking southeast towards Sv Mihovil

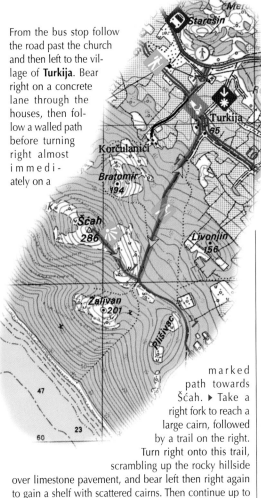

From the bus stop follow the road past the church and then left to the village of **Turkija**. Bear right on a concrete lane through the houses, then follow a walled path before turning right almost immediately on a marked path towards Šćah. ▸ Take a right fork to reach a large cairn, followed by a trail on the right. Turn right onto this trail, scrambling up the rocky hillside over limestone pavement, and bear left then right again to gain a shelf with scattered cairns. Then continue up to the summit of **Šćah** (286m), marked by a simple wooden cross, 70mins from the bus stop.

The trail straight ahead leads to Sutomišćica and Preko, and would provide a nice 'shortcut' to Sv Mihovil if it wasn't extremely overgrown in places.

There are excellent views of Paklenica and the Southern Velebit mountains beyond Zadar to the north-east, Sv Mihovil with the island of Pašman beyond to the

137

southeast, and Dugi otok and the Kornati islands to the west and south.

Return to **Turkija** and the bus stop by the same route (allow 45mins).

OTHER WALKS ON UGLJAN AND PAŠMAN

Sv Mihovil

From the tourist information office in Preko follow a narrow lane uphill to the main road, then go up a path on the opposite side and turn right onto the asphalt road to Sv Mihovil. There's a nice path down to a climbing area above Željina Bay, which makes up a bit for all the road walking – turn left onto a 4WD track just before reaching the summit/fort, then right onto a marked path. An old route from just below the fort directly across to Šćah, despite starting promisingly, is unfortunately so overgrown that it's very difficult to follow without flaying yourself among thorny bushes.

Veliki Bokolj (Pašman)

Since Ugljan and Pašman are connected by bridge and share the same bus service, it's easy to combine a visit to the two islands. Veliki Bokolj (274m), the highest point on Pašman, can be reached from the village of Dobropoljana (towards the northwest end of the island, on the main road and bus route) in around 45mins.

DUGI OTOK

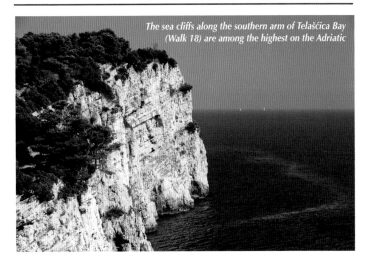

The sea cliffs along the southern arm of Telašćica Bay (Walk 18) are among the highest on the Adriatic

Dugi otok (which means 'long island' in Croatian) stretches for some 45km down the outer western edge of the Zadar archipelago. The island terminates at either end in a pair of long arms, with those in the south enclosing Telašćica Bay – at 8.2km long, one of the largest bays on the Adriatic – like a pair of oversized pincer claws. The bay and its surroundings form Telašćica Nature Park, a beautiful area that to the southeast blends imperceptibly into the myriad fragmented isles of the Kornati archipelago and the Kornati Islands National Park. The word 'Telašćica' is thought to derive from Latin *tri lagus* ('three lakes'), a reference to the various

spits and headlands along the shores of Telašćica Bay that almost divide it into three separate coves, and would have corresponded to three large karst depressions before the area became submerged below the Adriatic.

Much of Dugi otok's southwest coastline ends abruptly in a series of spectacular sea cliffs, which reach their highest at Grpašćak and Prisika on the west side of the southwestern arm of Telašćica Bay. Towards the tip of this southwestern arm is a large saltwater lake, Mir jezero (Walk 18), fed by underground channels. The main gateway to Telašćica is Sali, a remarkably quiet, unspoilt little fishing village just north of the park

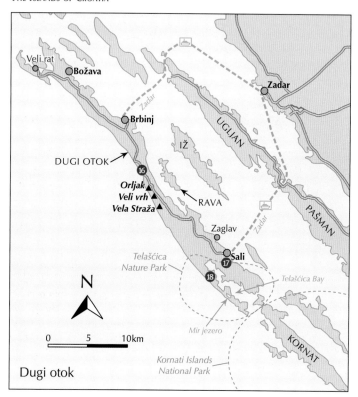

Dugi otok

boundary, surrounded by several low hills which make excellent viewpoints over the bay below (Walk 17). Several larger hills rise from the narrow central part of the island, the highest of them (Vela Straža, 338m) crowned by radio antennae and out of bounds, but the neighbouring Orljak (301m) and Veli vrh (328m) make for one of the best hikes on the Croatian Adriatic (Walk 16).

The island's most popular beach, Saharun, is in the north of the island, near the settlement of Božava. Further north still, towards the northern tip of the island, is the 19th-century lighthouse at Veli rat – at 42m the tallest on the Adriatic. The original paint for the lighthouse is said to have been mixed with some 100,000 egg yolks.

Visitors based in Sali (and for the walks in this guide, it does make most

A performance of Tovareća mužika on the waterfront in Sali

GETTING THERE AND GETTING AROUND

There's a daily passenger ferry between Zadar and Sali, calling at Zaglav on the return journey, and a catamaran makes the same journey three times a day (both www.gv-line.hr). Another ferry sails between Zadar and Brbinj in the north of the island (www.jadrolinija.hr); however, if you're planning to visit Sali and Telašćica nature park, do not take this ferry unless you have your own transport – there is no public transport running south from Brbinj to Sali and Telašćica (apart from a once-weekly bus service), although buses do run north from Brbinj to Božava.

This means that there is no public transport between Sali and Walk 16, so unless you have your own car the start of the walk is accessible only by taxi (Taxi Frka; tel. +385 (0)98 891 036; www.taxidugiotok.com), which will cost around 200kn for the return journey from Sali to the trailhead (arrange pick-up at specified time from trailhead). Since it's on the way to Saharun, there are very likely to be other passengers going that way. Similarly, there is no public transport to the start of Walk 18, although it's possible to walk from Sali. However, a taxi will cost only around 70kn per person, which includes the drive from Sali to the car park at the start of the walk and the return journey to Sali – agree a return time later in the day/evening (contact Taxi Frka, see above).

sense to be based there) should try to catch a performance of Tovareća mužika ('donkey music') – a traditional style of music, performed on cattle horns to a loud drumbeat, which is unique to the town of Sali.

TOURIST INFORMATION

The tourist information office in Sali is on the waterfront, on the opposite (south) side of the harbour from where the ferry arrives (Obala Petra Lorinja bb; tel. +385 (0)23 377 094; www.dugiotok.hr). The Zadar County Tourist Board also has plenty of useful information (Sv Leopolda B Mandia 1, Zadar; tel. +385 (023) 315 316; www.zadar.hr).

The trail to Oštravica (Walk 16)

ACCOMMODATION

Private accommodation can be booked through the tourist office in Sali. Apartmani Šošterić (tel. +385 (0)23 377 050) is recommended, a stone's throw from where the ferry docks.

MAPS

The HGSS are planning a new sheet, Dugi Otok – Tourist and Trekking Map (1:25,000), to be published in 2014. Otherwise, for Walks 17 and 18 there is Javna ustanova park prirode Telašćica (1:25,000), available from the tourist information office in Sali. The small, free 'Sali in your pocket' is also useful for Walk 17. The Dugi Otok – Trekking and Mountain Biking Map (1:30,000), also free, covers all three walks, but is much less detailed.

OTHER ESSENTIALS

An ATM, supermarkets and a pharmacy can be found in Sali. Bikes can be hired from the café/ice cream shop at the head of the harbour in Sali.

WALK 16

Oštravica, Orljak and Veli vrh

Start/Finish	Junction on the main Sali–Brbinj road, where 4WD track branches southwest to Strašna peć, around 17km north of Sali, 5.5km south of Savar (116m)
Distance	6km
Time	3hrs 10mins
Terrain	Steady climb on a clear, well-marked path. Final section of route between Orljak and Veli vrh is very rocky and slightly more demanding, with plenty of boulder-hopping.
Highest point	Veli vrh (328m)
Maps	Dugi Otok – Tourist and Trekking Map (HGSS); due to be published in 2014. In 2013 the free Dugi Otok – Trekking and Mountain Biking Map (1:30,000) didn't yet cover the whole route, although this is expected to change.
Access	No public transport to start of this walk, so book a taxi there and back (see 'Getting there and getting around')

A superb, clearly marked route along the rocky spine of Dugi otok, roughly at the island's narrow mid-point, taking in the three highpoints of Oštravica, Orljak and Veli vrh. Wonderful views and an excellent path – involving in its final section plenty of boulder-hopping over some wildly contorted and fractured limestone – combine with good opportunities for spotting mouflon to make this the best hike on Dugi otok.

From the **Sali–Brbinj road** turn left onto the 4WD track, following the signs to 'Orljak, Oštravica and Strašna peć', then turn left onto a clear, well-marked footpath. Shortly after reaching a saddle, arrive at a junction, 35mins from the main road. Turn left to reach the broad, rocky summit of **Oštravica** (275m) in 10mins.

> The **views** from Oštravica are superb, taking in the entire northwestern extent of island; the view southeast across Vela Straža (the highest point on Dugi otok), with its antennae, to Sali and the scattered

143

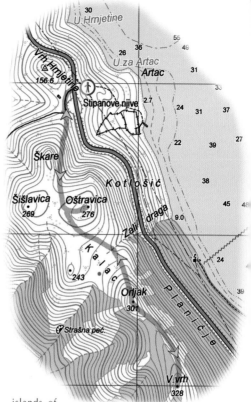

islands of
the Kornati
archipelago; and a sweep northeast across the small
islands of Rava and Mali Iž to Ugljan, with its two
prominent peaks, Sv Mihovil (the one with the
antennae) and, to the left of this, Šćah (Walk 15).
There's a fish farm in the bay below, where species
such as gilthead bream and sea bass are bred.

Return to the junction below Oštravica and turn left,
descending gradually on a lovely path over broad, open
slopes, scented with wild sage and other herbs. Keep
an eye out for mouflon (wild sheep) on the surrounding

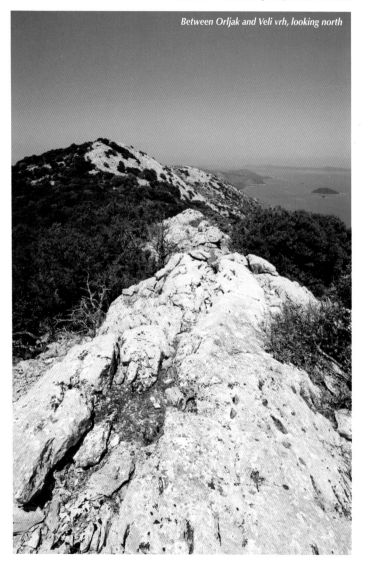

Between Orljak and Veli vrh, looking north

Orljak

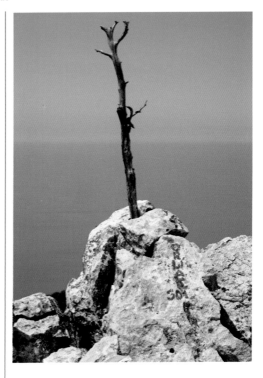

Strašna peć is a cave which, like Pećina Vlakno slightly further north along the coast, was inhabited or at least used by early humans during the Neolithic period.

slopes. P⁔s a trail to Strašna peć on the right. ◄ Then head ste⸱ly uphill to reach the summit of **Orljak** (301m), 40mins from the junction with the trail to Oštravica. As with Ostravica, the views from Orljak are excellent, and Southern swallowtail and Two-tailed pasha butterflies flit and dart around the summit cairn.

From Orljak the route (marked 'vrh') continues over a spectacularly rocky section with plenty of boulder-hopping to reach the rock-strewn summit of **Veli vrh** (328m) in 25mins.

Retrace your steps over Orljak and past Oštravica to reach the **main road** in 75mins.

WALK 17
Kruševac

Start/Finish	Tourist information office, Sali (1m)
Distance	3km
Time	1hr
Terrain	Mostly on asphalt and unsealed road, followed by short rocky path (unmarked but reasonably clear) and some boulder-hopping at the summit
Highest point	Kruševac (156m)
Maps	Javna ustanova park prirode Telašćica (1:25,000). Dugi Otok – Tourist and Trekking Map (HGSS); due to be published in 2014. The free Dugi otok – Trekking and Mountain Biking Map (1:30,000) doesn't mark this route or the 4WD track it partially follows
Note	There are plans afoot to clear and trailblaze the old, little-used paths on this and other hills around Sali – check at the tourist information office for details.

A short, easy walk to Kruševac, one of several low hills which surround the small fishing village of Sali. Kruševac lies on the boundary of Telašćica Nature Park, and commands clear views over the beautiful Telašćica Bay and the scattered islands of the Kornati archipelago.

From the tourist information office in **Sali**, turn right along the waterfront (walking away from the town centre), then

Telašćica Bay from Kruševac

turn right up a flight of steps. Turn left on the main road, walking uphill, and take the second road on the left, by a memorial to the Partisans and opposite the 'Put Masline' ('olive road'). Take the first road on the right and follow this uphill.

Just before the crest of the hill, turn left onto an unmarked, overgrown path between two walls, then follow an unmarked (although clear enough) rocky trail through forest and maquis, veering right and uphill. Some 30mins from Sali, emerge onto the rocky top of **Kruševac** (156m), with views across Telašćica Bay and the islands of the Kornati archipelago.

Descend to **Sali** by the same route (allow 30mins).

WALK 18

Telašćica Bay and Mir jezero

Start/Finish	Car park at end of road towards Mir jezero (30m); or Tourist information office, Sali (1m)
Distance	6.5km; or 23.5km
Time	1hr 30mins; or 5hrs 10mins
Terrain	Broad, well-used track, with a short uphill stretch on an easy path on the main route; starting from Sali includes a fairly long stretch on asphalt
Highest point	50m; or 125m
Maps	Javna ustanova park prirode Telašćica (1:25,000). Dugi Otok – Tourist and Trekking Map (HGSS); due to be published in 2014. Mir jezero is sometimes written 'Jezero Mir' on maps.
Access	No public transport to the start of the main route, so book a taxi there and back (see 'Getting there and getting around' for notes on booking a taxi and for notes on accessing the alternative start/finish at Sali)
Entrance fees	Entrance to Telašćica Nature Park is 25kn. Buy tickets from kiosk at park boundary on road towards Mir jezero from Sali. Anyone walking or cycling from Sali will turn off main road before reaching kiosk, so buy tickets at cafés just before Mir jezero.

A short, very easy walk to the most popular area of Telašćica Nature Park, visiting impressive sea cliffs and the large saltwater lake Mir jezero.

Instead of taking a taxi to the trailhead, an alternative is to walk there from Sali. This involves a fairly long (1hr 50mins each way) although not unpleasant road walk, mostly on asphalt but with a short section of 4WD track.

Alternative start at Sali

Turn left from the tourist information office in **Sali** towards the head of the harbour, then turn left up a side street just before the ice cream café. Pass a church on the right, then turn right onto the main road, then after a couple of paths on the left to Berčastac take a 4WD track on the left marked 'Telašćica' with a picture of a bicycle. Some 45mins from Sali turn left at a junction (again marked 'Telašćica') onto the road, then left at the next junction

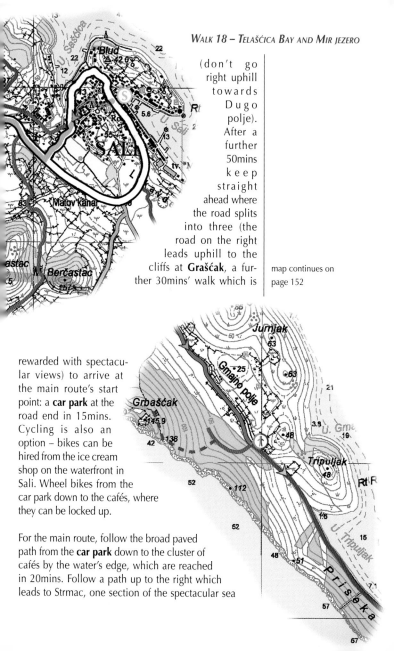

(don't go right uphill towards Dugo polje). After a further 50mins keep straight ahead where the road splits into three (the road on the right leads uphill to the cliffs at **Grašćak**, a fur-ther 30mins' walk which is

map continues on page 152

rewarded with spectacu-lar views) to arrive at the main route's start point: a car park at the road end in 15mins. Cycling is also an option – bikes can be hired from the ice cream shop on the waterfront in Sali. Wheel bikes from the car park down to the cafés, where they can be locked up.

For the main route, follow the broad paved path from the **car park** down to the cluster of cafés by the water's edge, which are reached in 20mins. Follow a path up to the right which leads to Strmac, one section of the spectacular sea

Mir jezero

Instead of turning left to follow the path above the cliffs, at this point walkers can return to the main path by the cafés and turn right to reach Mir jezero.

From the far (south) side of the lake it's possible to continue a further 1km to Skrača Bay and Lojišć, a popular beach (often used by naturists).

cliffs which run along the island's southwest coast. Turn left along a sometimes faint path running above the cliffs, then descend left to reach the lake **Mir jezero**. ◄

Mir jezero (the name means 'peace lake') is a salt-water lake fed by underground karst channels. There are quite a few donkeys in the area around the lake – although there has been talk of fencing them off, since over the years they've discovered that visitors like to feed them, and when visitors neglect to do so, they've been known to steal food and to bite in protest!

Follow the path around the lake. ◄ At the northwest end of the lake follow a path that leads back to the cafés without following the cliff path. From the cafés return to the car park by the same route.

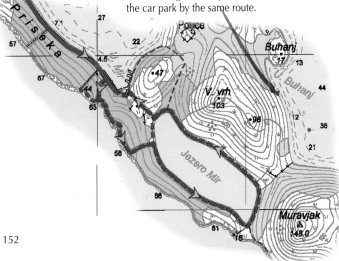

BRAČ

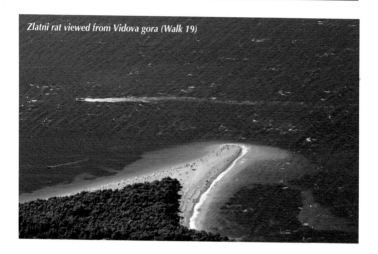

Zlatni rat viewed from Vidova gora (Walk 19)

Croatia's third largest island, Brač lies around 12km offshore from Split, separated from its nearest neighbour, Šolta, by a narrow straight, Splitska vrata, which is the main shipping channel in the area. Brač is one of the most popular holiday spots on the Croatian Adriatic, in particular the small town of Bol on the island's south coast, which just happens to be next to Croatia's most famous beach, Zlatni rat – a long spit of fine golden shingle backed by pines. Its tip is ever changing into a slightly different shape with the action of the strong currents between Brač and its even more popular neighbour, Hvar, to the south.

Bol and Zlatni rat are backed by the crags of Vidova gora (780m, Walk 19), the highest point on Brač – and of any island on the Croatian Adriatic. The main town on the island, Supetar (birthplace of one of Croatia's famous sculptors, Ivan Rendić), is on the north coast, and the small town of Milna (birthplace of Croatian tennis hero and former Wimbledon champion Goran Ivanišević) is on the west coast of the island – but outside these spots the still largely rural central part of the island sees relatively few visitors.

Well worth visiting while on Brač is Pustinja Blaca, a monastery hidden away on a remote and rocky hillside above the island's southwest coast.

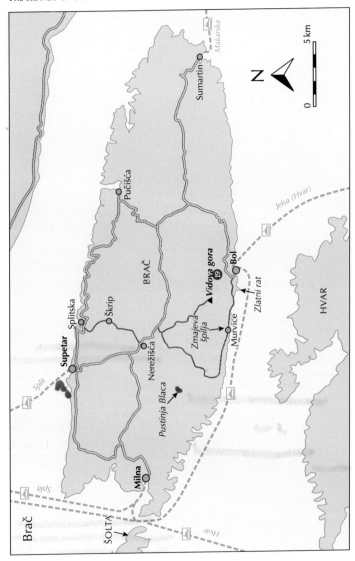

founded by Glagolitic monks in the 16th century. Originally from Poljica (an area on the mainland, behind the mountains which rise just inland from Split), the monks arrived on the island after being displaced by the Ottomans, and initially settled in a cave near the village of Murvice, around 4km west from Zlatni rat. Known as Zmajeva špilja ('dragon's cave'), the cave is decorated with an intriguing series of stone carvings – a medley of religious figures, cultic symbols, gargoyles and other monstrosities – and can be visited. There are boat trips from Bol to a bay on the coast below Pustinja Blaca, from where there's a path up

The small church of Sv Ivana i Teodora (St Ivan and Theodore), the oldest church in Bol

to the monastery, or a visit could be included on one of the island's well-developed cycle routes. A local guide (contact Zoran Kojdić, tel. +385 (0)91 514 9787) takes visitors up to Zmajeva špilja from the village of Murvice. The cave is kept locked. Škrip – the oldest settlement on the island, near Supetar – is also worth visiting, and is home to the Museum of Brač.

TOURIST INFORMATION

The tourist information office in Supetar is directly opposite where the ferry moors (Porat 10; tel. +385 (0)21 630 900; www.supetar.hr); the tourist information office in Bol is on the waterfront, near where the catamaran arrives (Porat bolskih pomoraca bb; tel. +385 (0)21 635 638; www.bol.hr).

GETTING THERE AND GETTING AROUND

There's a frequent ferry service between Split and Supetar, and a daily catamaran from Split to Bol, continuing to Jelsa on the island of Hvar; another daily catamaran stops at Milna on its route between Split and Hvar town (all www.jadrolinija.hr). There's also a car ferry between Sumartin, in the east of the island, and Makarska on the mainland.

A regular bus service links the towns of Supetar and Bol, usually via Pučišća; another, less frequent service goes from Supetar to Nerežišća, and there are also buses from Supetar to

Windsurfing near Zlatni rat

Škrip. In Supetar, buses depart from just east of the ferry dock and tourist information office (when you get off the ferry, turn left – don't go straight ahead around the harbour – and the bus station will be on your right). In Bol, the bus station is on the waterfront, walking away from the old town towards Zlatni rat. For timetables see www.autotrans.hr.

ACCOMMODATION

Private accommodation is listed on the Supetar and Bol Tourist Board websites (www.supetar.hr and www. bol.hr), and can also be booked through Vakance (www.bracinfo.com) and other agencies.

MAPS

The most detailed map of the island is the newly published Brač Bike – Bike Tourist Map (HGSS, 1:45,000), available from the tourist information offices in Supetar and Bol.

OTHER ESSENTIALS

An ATM, supermarkets and pharmacies can be found in either Supetar or Bol. Bikes can be rented from Big Blue Sport (www.bigbluesport.com) on the promenade between Bol and Zlatni rat (there is also a windsurfing school here, one of the best spots for windsurfing in Croatia) and in Supetar (www.rent-a-bike-brac.com).

WALK 19
Vidova gora

Start/Finish	Main road just above Bol, by street called Donje Podbarje (105m)
Distance	7.5km
Time	3hrs 30mins
Terrain	Straightforward ascent on a clear rocky path/track, although minimal shade makes it better walked early in the day; short section on asphalt at the beginning/end
Highest point	Vidova gora (780m)
Maps	Brač Bike – Bike Tourist Map (HGSS, 1:45,000)
Access	Regular bus service between Supetar and Bol. If coming from Supetar, ask to be dropped off at turnoff to Vidova gora (say 'Za Vidova gora'), where Donje Podbarje turns inland off main road. Bus for return journey leaves from bus station on the waterfront.

A classic hike to the highest point on any of the islands, with wonderful views. Plenty of ascent, and trail markings only appear near the top of the route – but the path is very clear and easy to follow throughout.

▶ From the Vidova gora sign on the main road above **Bol**, walk up Donje Podbarje and keep straight ahead where the road peters out into a 4WD track and then a path. The trail soon zigzags up to the right, with good views of Velo Koštilo, the rocky hill on the left. Around 50mins from the main road the trail passes a large cairn and crosses to the opposite (left) side of the valley, going under the pylons briefly. Pass a small sinkhole on the left, the mouth of which is right beside the path, then turn right onto a very rough 4WD track. Turn left at the wire fence (which is where the trail markings start), and follow a path along the top of the cliff to the car park. Beyond the car park follow the asphalted road up to the antennae, buildings and generators on the summit of **Vidova gora** (780m), 1hr 50mins from the main road.

If staying in Bol – walk up Novi put, which joins main road directly opposite Donje Podbarje.

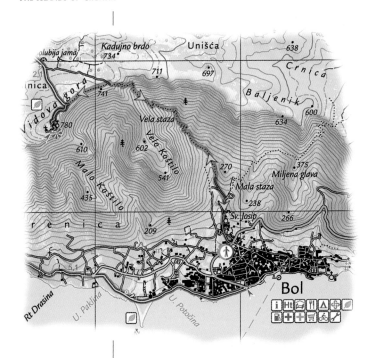

There are excellent **views** down over Bol and Zlatni rat to the Kabal peninsula on the island of Hvar, with its wildly indented coastline, particularly from the cliff tops just beyond the summit. There's also a nice little konoba (Konoba Vidova gora) serving wild boar goulash and other dishes, as well as Turkish coffee, beer and other drinks. A small plaque on the stone wall surrounding the antennae and buildings on the summit commemorates the British Armed Forces who fought and died on Brač and other Dalmatian islands during the Second World War.

Return to the main road in **Bol** by the same route (allow 90mins).

To reach the waterfront and bus station in the centre of Bol itself, continue down the street directly opposite Donje Podbarje to the waterfront (10mins). If you plan to go to Zlatni rat, it's more direct to turn right onto the main road at the bottom of Donje Podbarje and follow this downhill, then where the road turns sharply left keep straight ahead down an alley to reach the seaside promenade between Bol and Zlatni rat, and turn right.

Approaching the summit of Vidova gora, with Zlatni rat in the distance below

HVAR

Cyclists on Stari Grad Plain (Walk 21)

South of Brač across the Hvarski kanal (Hvar channel), and tapering into a long narrow 'tail' which terminates only around 4.5km off the mainland, Hvar has long been considered among the most glamorous destinations on the islands and boasts more days of sunshine than anywhere else on the Adriatic.

Of the three main towns on the island, Hvar, Stari Grad and Jelsa, it is Hvar town that sees the lion's share of visitors. However, it was at Paros, modern Stari Grad, that the Greeks settled in the fourth century BC, cultivating the fertile land of the broad plain just to the east of their settlement. The agricultural landscape of

this plain has remained little changed for the past two and a half millennia – grapes and olives are still grown here as they were by the Greeks and Romans, and the land is divided by a geometrical grid of drystone walls and tracks according to the ancient Greek system of land division, the *chora*. These rectangular plots (around 180m x 900m) were further subdivided in medieval times. Stari Grad Plain (Walk 21) is now a UNESCO Word Heritage Site (Croatia has several UNESCO-listed sites, but Stari Grad Plain is the **only** one on the islands).

Settlement on the island goes back at least to the Neolithic period, and Grapčeva špilja, a cave near the

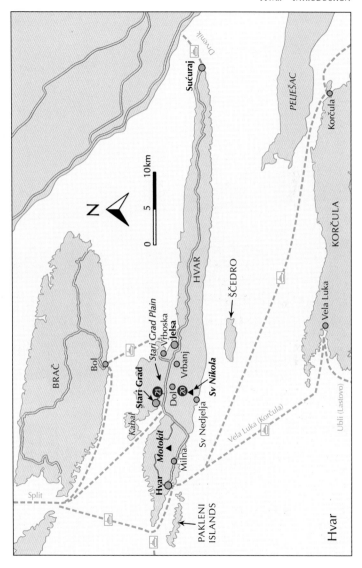

Hvar

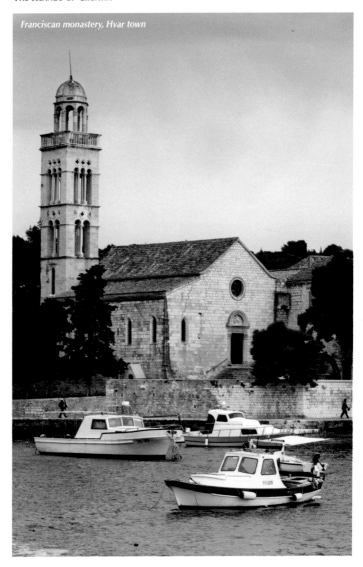

Franciscan monastery, Hvar town

village of Humac bristling with stalagmites and stalactites, was used by Neolithic people as a place of cultic worship.

South of Stari Grad Plain, beyond the villages of Dol and Vrbanj, the land rises steadily to an extended ridge of hills, the highest point of which, Sv Nikola (628m, Walk 20), commands jaw-dropping views stretching on a clear day to the heel of Italy. Vineyards towards the bottom of the steep cliffs below this ridge, particularly those at Ivan dolac, produce some of the best red wine on the islands.

Traditional lace-making in Hvar town, along with that made on the island of Pag and at Lepoglava in northern Croatia, is inscribed on the UNESCO List of Intangible Cultural Heritage. On Hvar the lace is unusual in that it is made from agave threads, a technique practised by Benedictine nuns for centuries. Za križem, a series of six religious processions between the villages of Jelsa, Vrboska, Vrbanj, Pitke, Vrisnik and Svirče during the night following Maundy Thursday, is also inscribed on the same UNESCO list.

TOURIST INFORMATION

The tourist information office in Stari Grad is on the waterfront at the head of the town's long natural harbour, a 5min walk northwest of the bus station (Obala dr. Franje Tuđmana 1; tel. +385 (0)21 765 763; www. stari-grad-faros.hr).

GETTING THERE AND GETTING AROUND

There's a ferry from Split to Stari Grad several times a day (www.jadrolinija. hr), and Hvar town is served by several different catamaran routes – one continuing to Vela Luka and Ubli (on the islands of Korčula and Lastovo respectively), another to Korčula town, one arriving via Milna on the island of Brač (all www.jadrolinija. hr), and another just between Split and Hvar town (www.krilo.hr). There's also a weekly ferry service between Rijeka and Dubrovnik (www.jadrolinija.hr), calling at Split, Hvar and Korčula town. Another catamaran route links the town of Jelsa with Split, calling at Bol on the island of Brač, and a car ferry runs from Sućuraj, at the far eastern point of Hvar, to Drvenik on the mainland (both www.jadrolinija.hr).

A good local bus service runs between Hvar town, Stari Grad and Jelsa, and another runs between the ferry dock for Stari Grad and the town itself, around 2.5km away (for timetables see www.stari-grad-faros. hr). The bus station in Stari Grad is on the southeastern side of the town – to get to the town centre and the tourist information office turn left (west) from the bus station alongside the park.

ACCOMMODATION

For private accommodation in and around Stari Grad see the local tourist

163

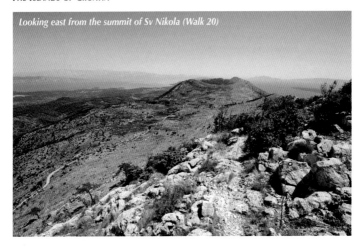
Looking east from the summit of Sv Nikola (Walk 20)

board website (www.stari-grad-faros.hr) or contact Hvar Turistik in Stari Grad (www.hvar-touristik.com).

MAPS

Hvar Tourist and Trekking Map (HGSS, 1:25,000) – Zapad (West); this sheet is available from the tourist information office in Stari Grad. The accompanying Istok (East) sheet has not yet been published, but the reverse of the West sheet covers the whole island at 1:40,000. For exploring Stari Grad Plain, whether on foot or by bike, the best map is Starogradsko polje (Stari Grad Plain), available free from the tourist information office in Stari Grad (no scale), who also produce several handy maps of local bike routes (Ager, Eko and Kabal routes).

OTHER ESSENTIALS

ATMs, supermarkets and pharmacies can be found in Stari Grad, Hvar town, Jelsa, Vrboska and other centres. For bike rental in Stari Grad head for KGM, between the tourist information office and the bus station.

WALK 20
Sv Nikola

Start	Tourist information office, Stari Grad (1m)
Finish	Vrbanj (100m)
Distance	17.5km
Time	5hrs
Terrain	Asphalt then almost entirely 4WD track, with rocky path over the summit
Highest point	Sv Nikola (628m)
Maps	Hvar Tourist and Trekking Map (HGSS, 1:25,000) – West sheet (Zapad). Route from just east of Sv Nikola down to Vrbanj is on (unpublished) East sheet, but 1:40,000 island map on reverse of West sheet covers this area.
Access	Regular bus service between Hvar, Stari Grad, Vrboska and Jelsa. Bus also passes the turnoff to Dol – get off here to avoid initial walk along main road from Stari Grad. **Note** There are two Dols – ask to be dropped off at turnoff to Dol Sv Marije, the turnoff closest to main Stari Grad–Jelsa road.

A hike to highest point on the island of Hvar, Sv Nikola – an outstandingly beautiful spot and one of the most spectacular viewpoints on the Adriatic. This is one of the few routes in the guide to be mostly on 4WD tracks rather than footpaths, but a large part of the way up is through forest, which makes for pleasant walking shaded from the relentless heat.

From the tourist information office in **Stari Grad**, walk back along the road to the bus station and turn right, then left, then right to reach the main Hvar–Jelsa road. Turn left onto the main road (some caution required – there's a lot of traffic in the summer and no pavement), passing a trail on the right to Purkin kuk. ▶ Then turn right onto the road to Dol. Take the right fork where the road splits (straight ahead would lead to Vrbanj) and walk uphill through the scattered houses of **Dol Sv Marije**. Bear left and uphill around a sharp bend as the church comes into view, then

Purkin kuk is a nice little peak, the site of an Illyrian hill fort, with great views of Stari Grad Plain, although the path from here tends to get lost among the olive groves.

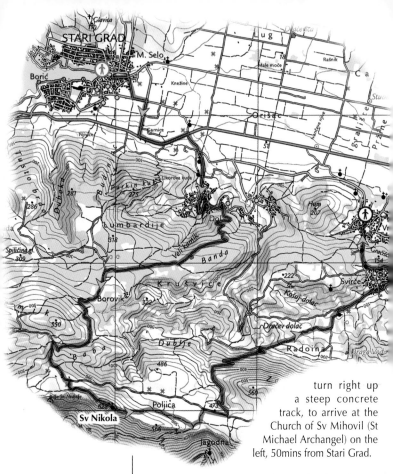

turn right up a steep concrete track, to arrive at the Church of Sv Mihovil (St Michael Archangel) on the left, 50mins from Stari Grad.

There has been a **church** on this spot since at least the 14th century, although the present building dates from 1910. The altar and late 16th-century altarpiece from the earlier church are inside, and there are excellent views of Vidova gora on the island of Brač from the terrace.

Walk straight ahead from the church (turn right at the top of the concrete track), then go straight ahead on a

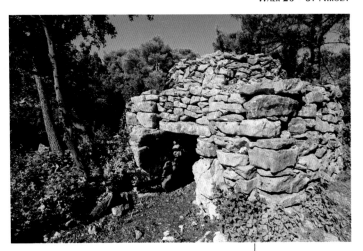

4WD track which zigzags steeply up through the forest. Some 30mins from the church pass a well-preserved *trim* on the left.

Traditional stone shelter (or trim) on the 4WD road above Dol

> The **trim** (pronounced 'treem') is a characteristic feature of the island. These drystone shelters, with a vaulted roof and built without the use of any form of cement, were once widespread, their form and construction probably having remained unchanged for millennia, although the latest ones may have been built around the end of the 19th century.

Pass a small well on the left. The prominent hill straight ahead is not Sv Nikola but Remik, but Sv Nikola soon appears to the left of this. The surrounding slopes become more open, scattered with fallen trees, then 1hr 20mins from Dol reach a broad saddle and a junction, where a 4WD road branches off to the right to Dubovica (and continues all the way to Sv Nedjelja, without going through a tunnel, unlike the main road further east). Turn left and continue uphill to reach Konoba Kolumbić on the right. ▶

This is a lovely little konoba, perfectly placed for a lunch stop, particularly if you plan to return to Stari Grad from Sv Nikola by the same route instead of continuing to Svirče.

167

The large cross on Sv Nikola summit

Take the right fork of the 4WD road, then pass one arm of the circular trail up from Sv Nedjelja (see 'Other walks on Hvar'; page 172), before ascending steeply past the fire-watch station to the large cross and tiny church on the airy summit ridge of **Sv Nikola** (628m), 2hrs from Dol.

The **views** from Sv Nikola are nothing short of phenomenal. On a clear day (and Hvar does, famously, have more of those than anywhere else on the Croatian Adriatic) the remote island of Palagruža and heel of Italy are visible. Less distant landmarks include the Pelješac peninsula and the islands of Šćedro and Korčula to the southeast, with Lastovo just visible beyond, Vis to the southwest, the Pakleni Islands along the coast to the west, and the small town of Sv Nedjelja sitting at the bottom of a wall of cliffs below. The church, also called Sv Nikola, was built in 1459, but has been destroyed by lightning and rebuilt several times since then.

Continue east from the church, descending and turning left (the path straight ahead goes down to Sv Nedjelja, see 'Other walks on Hvar') to the 4WD road.

Turn right onto this, then 30mins from Sv Nikola turn left at a junction, following the 4WD road downhill towards Svirče. ▶ Arrive at a small chapel on the left, 50mins from Sv Nikola. Walk down to the church then follow a path to the right, rejoining the 4WD road and turning left, and soon passing another church on a sharp corner. Pass another small church on the right before arriving at the houses of **Svirče**, 1hr 40mins from Sv Nikola. Bear right on the road (signposted to Jelsa), then turn left at the junction to arrive at the large, prominent church, Sv Magdalena (built in the 20th century), at the far end of the village.

Walk back along the road a short distance then go straight ahead (signposted 'za Vrbanj') where the road bends left and turn right up a narrow concrete, then cobbled, lane. Go straight ahead on a track then downhill, passing a shrine on the left, then bear right to arrive at the main square in **Vrbanj**, 20mins from Svirče, where there are a couple of welcome cafés. To get to the bus stop, follow the road on the far side of the square to the crossroads, by the Church of the Holy Spirit (Sv Duh). Make sure you're visible to the driver and flag the bus down.

An easily missed path on the left, before reaching the junction, provides a shortcut: turn left onto the 4WD track at the bottom of the path.

Small church between Sv Nikola and Vrbanj

WALK 21
Stari Grad Plain

Start/Finish	Tourist information office, Stari Grad (1m)
Distance	9km
Time	2hrs
Terrain	Short section on asphalt then mostly on unsealed road, and briefly on a clear path at the end; minimal height gain
Highest point	Maslinovik (65m)
Maps	Starogradsko polje (Stari Grad Plain) (no scale). Stari Grad Plain area also covered in less detail on reverse of Hvar Tourist and Trekking Map (HGSS, 1:40,000) – West sheet (Zapad).
Access	Regular bus service between Hvar, Stari Grad, Vrboska and Jelsa

An easy walk through Stari Grad Plain (a UNESCO World Heritage Site), cultivated by the Greeks in the fourth century BC and little changed for some two and a half millennia. The walk follows 4WD tracks and one short footpath to the site of an ancient watch tower. The tracks and drystone walls preserve the original Greek system of land division, known as the *chora*. The walk is also popular as a cycle route.

From the tourist information office in **Stari Grad**, walk back along the road past the bus station, then straight ahead past an electrical substation onto an unsealed road, passing the small Gospojica (Church of Our Lady), built in the 16th century by a local nobleman, on the left.

The unsealed road, **Put Demetrija Farskog**, runs in a straight line through the centre of Stari Grad Plain. It is named after Dimitrius of Pharos, one of the most powerful figures in the region, who during the third century BC was an ally of the Illyrian Queen Teuta, whom Rome attacked in 229BC, the date which marks the beginning of the Roman conquest of Illyria. The junction of Put Demetrija

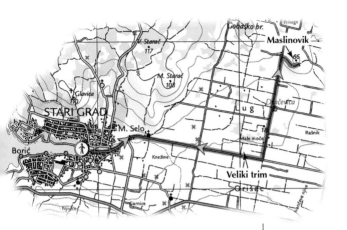

Farskog and Matijev put – known as Omphalos ('navel of the plain') – marks the point from which the Greeks measured and began their land division of the plain.

Between the junctions of two more 4WD tracks running perpendicular to Put Demetrija Farskog (Komonov put and Matijev put) there is a small, round stone shelter, known as a **trim**. These drystone shelters, with a vaulted roof and built without the use of any form of cement, were once widespread, their form and construction probably having remained unchanged for millennia, although the latest ones may have been built around the end of the 19th century. This one is quite well preserved and is usually known as Veliki trim ('big trim').

Turn left along Matijev put, walking very slightly downhill past Rašnik, a small hamlet which, like many in the area, was abandoned in the second half of the 20th century, although a couple of families have now returned. Further along Matijev put a small marshy area, **Dračevica**, is passed, also on the right. ▶ Continue along Matijev put, slightly uphill, then turn right onto a footpath. After 5mins arrive at a group of ruined stone houses and turn left to reach Maslinovik, 1hr from Stari Grad.

This is the only surface-water spring, and probably site of the earliest human settlement, on Stari Grad Plain.

Maslinovik, site of an ancient Greek watchtower on Stari Grad Plain

Maslinovik was the site of a fourth-century BC Greek watchtower, and there are similar towers on Purkin kuk (near Dol) and Tor (near Jelsa). The foundations of the tower have been excavated, and although the hill is only 67m above sea level there are good views out across Stari Grad Plain to Vrbanj, Dol and Sv Nikola (Walk 20).

Return to **Stari Grad** by the same route.

OTHER WALKS ON HVAR

Sv Nedjelja to Sv Nikola

This is arguably the most spectacular route to the top of Sv Nikola, zigzagging up over the almost sheer slopes from the small town of Sv Nedjelja below. However Sv Nedjelja is difficult to get to without a car – the bus only goes once a week, and the main road goes through a long tunnel under the mountain and is not recommended for cyclists or pedestrians. (To cycle to Sv Nedjelja, follow

the 4WD road via Dubovica, which doesn't go through a tunnel – see Walk 20). There are two paths up, so it makes a good circular route, passing a cave (Špilja Sv Nedjelja) and small church (Gospa od Zdravlja) on the western 'arm'. Konoba Kolumbić, just a 5min detour (see Walk 20) away, makes a handy spot for lunch.

Sv Nikola, the highest point on the island of Hvar, can also be reached from Sv Nedjelja

Hvar to Milna, Motokit and V Grablje
Following the waterfront promenade around the headland south of Hvar town, it's possible to continue along the coast to Milna, from where a 4WD road can be followed to the village of M Grablje and a path to a nearby hill, Motokit (334m).

VIS

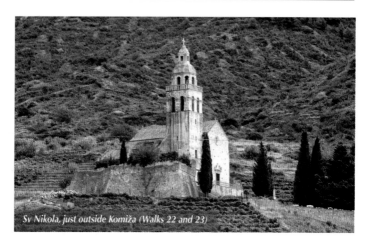

Sv Nikola, just outside Komiža (Walks 22 and 23)

The small island of Vis, one of the furthest inhabited islands from the Croatian coast, is also one of its most captivating. The two main settlements, Vis town and Komiža, sit in large bays at opposite ends of the island, but are only a 15min bus ride apart, while the rest of island has only a scattering of small villages, and the coastline is dotted with small coves. The centre of the island, in particular its western half, is quite mountainous, with the slopes of Hum (Walks 22 and 23), the highest peak on the island, making an outstanding hiking area.

The Greeks founded their first colony on the Adriatic here – Issa, modern Vis town – in the fourth century BC, fishing the surrounding waters in a distinctive type of narrow boat, the *falkuša*. It was these colonists from Vis who went on to found further colonies at Trogir and elsewhere on the Croatian coast and islands.

One particular historical anomaly of the island is that Vis was a British possession between 1811 and 1814. Vis was a key Adriatic possession during the Napoleonic Wars, and the forts built by the British – Fort Wellington, above the northeast headland of Vis Bay, and Fort George, above its western shores – are still there (the latter has recently been renovated and converted into an arts venue). Another British legacy is the game of cricket, introduced to the island by Captain William Hoste of Britain's Royal Navy,

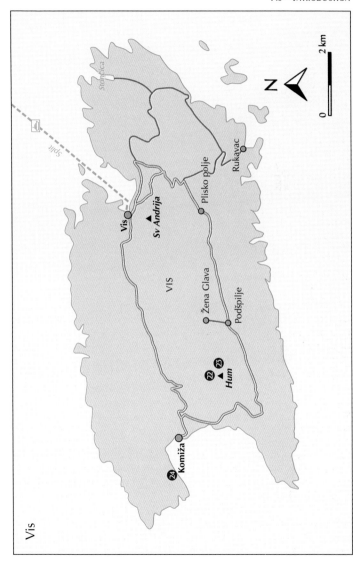

Vis

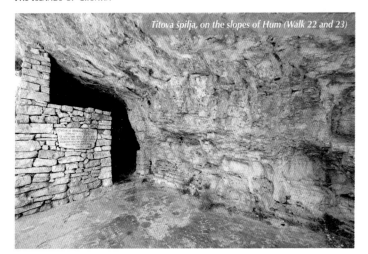
Titova špilja, on the slopes of Hum (Walk 22 and 23)

which is played on a former Second World War airstrip near Plisko polje.

Towards the end of the Second World War Josip Broz Tito, leader of the Partisans and later President of Yugoslavia, had his base on Vis, in a natural cave (Titova špilja) hidden away in the mountainous centre of the island. The island remained a naval base under Yugoslavia and was off limits to foreigners (with the exception of British veterans, who still hold a memorial service here in September) until 1989, when it finally opened to tourism. This goes a long way towards explaining the island's relatively underdeveloped, unspoilt character.

Boat trips to Modra špilja, the so-called 'Blue cave' on the small island of Biševo off the southwest coast of Vis, are popular. Here (at least, under the right weather and lighting conditions) the inside of the cave is bathed in shimmering blue light reflected off the sea floor. Anyone visiting the island of Vis on St Nicholas' Day (6 December) should make a point of being in Komiža, where locals drag a wooden fishing boat up to the church of Sv Nikola (St Nicholas) – and sacrificially burn it in honour of the patron saint of children and fishermen. The island's signature wine is Vugava viška, a crisp white.

TOURIST INFORMATION

The tourist information office in Vis town is on the waterfront directly opposite where the ferry and catamaran dock (Šetalište Stare Isse 5; tel. +385 (0)21 717 017; www.tz-vis.hr; the 'list of walking trails' descriptions on this website were in need of an update at the time of writing and did not always reflect trail conditions on the ground). The tourist information office in Komiža is on the waterfront (Riva Sv Mikule 2; tel. +385 (0)21 713 455; www.tz-komiza.hr).

GETTING THERE AND GETTING AROUND

Vis town can be reached from Split by either ferry (www.jadrolinija.hr), twice daily, or by catamaran (www.krilo.hr), daily, the latter calling at Hvar on Tuesdays.

A good local bus service runs along the 'new' road between Vis town and Komiža several times a day (Walks 22 and 24), with a journey time of around 15mins. There's a less regular service (every other day) along the 'old' road via Marine Zemlje and Podšpilje (Walk 23) – for timetables see www.tz-vis.hr.

ACCOMMODATION

Pansion Dionis (www.dionis.hr) is a decent little family-run pension in the centre of Vis town. For private accommodation see the Vis Tourist Board website (www.tz-vis.hr) or book through Paiz Travel in Vis town (www.paiz-travel.com). Kuća Visoka is a beautifully renovated old stone house in Vis town (www.thisisvis.com, minimum four-night stay). For places to stay outside Vis town

or Komiža, contact WearActive in Rukavac, on the island's rugged southern coast (www.wearactive.com). There's also a mountain hut near Vis town, Planinarska kuća Sv Andrija (www.hpd-hum.hr/planinarska_kuca), usually open at weekends during summer.

MAPS

Otok Vis Tourist and Trekking Map (HGSS, 1:20,000) is available from the tourist information office in Vis town or the small kiosk/newsagent next door. A less detailed map of the footpaths on the island (available free from the tourist information office) is also useful.

OTHER ESSENTIALS

There are ATMs, supermarkets and pharmacies in both Vis and Komiža. Buses for Komiža depart from the waterfront in Vis town, at the point where the ferry and catamaran arrive. The best restaurant on the island is undoubtedly the excellent Pojoda (tel. +385 (0)21 711 575), in Kut, about a 15min walk around the waterfront from the centre of Vis town; and the best pizzeria is Karijola (tel. +385 (0)21 711 433), about halfway around the waterfront towards Kut. For bike rental try Vis Special (www.vis-special.com) in Vis town.

WALK 22
Sv Mihovil to Sv Duh (Hum) and Komiža

Start	Sv Mihovil, a small church on the main Vis–Komiža road (300m)
Finish	Komiža (<5m)
Distance	7.5km
Time	3hrs 15mins
Terrain	Good rocky paths throughout; slightly steeper on descent to Komiža, with very short section of road walking at either end of route
Highest point	Sv Duh (563m)
Maps	Otok Vis Tourist and Trekking Map (HGSS, 1:20,000)
Access	Regular bus service between Vis and Komiža leaves from where ferry arrives in Vis and from Ul Hrvatskih Mučenika (by post office) in Komiža. Morning bus from Vis 07.00 (daily) or 08.30 (Mon/Wed/Fri). It travels northern road between Vis and Komiža (bus service on southern road doesn't go to start of this route). Ask to be dropped at Sv Mihovil, at last bend in road before it zigzags down to Komiža (say 'Prije serpentine').
Note	There's no official bus stop at Sv Mihovil, but drivers are usually happy to drop off there – although they may not be able to pick up there (the nearest 'official' stops are either further back down the road towards Vis or in Komiža itself).

The best hike on Vis, visiting two old churches on the Vis–Komiža road before climbing to Sv Duh, a small church just below the summit of Hum with outstanding views down over the Bay of Komiža. It is not possible to climb to the summit of Hum, which is a restricted military area with radar and antennae, and should not be approached under any circumstances – keep to the path instead. However, Sv Duh is only a few metres below the summit and much more pleasant, uncluttered by antennae and with unrestricted views. The walk can also be undertaken from Komiža – a trail winds upwards just north (left) of the main road and takes around 40mins.

From **Sv Mihovil**, follow the marked trail parallel to the road (which involves walking back towards Vis) before crossing the road where marked, around 100m before

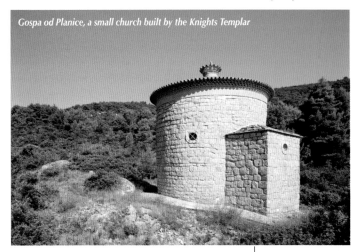
Gospa od Planice, a small church built by the Knights Templar

another small church, Gospa od Planice. Before striking out on the marked footpath on the opposite (south) side of the road, it's worth continuing along the road to **Gospa od Planice**. ▶

The church is on the opposite side of the road from which it is marked on the free map published by the local tourist board.

> The small church of **Sv Mihovil** dates from the 12th century, with 14th- and 16th-century renovations, and was initially the property of Benedictine monks from the nearby island of Bišovo. The distinctive circular building of **Gospa od Planice** is a church dating from the 11th century, although now much restored, founded by the Knights Templar.

Return to the trail markings and head SE and then south on a good path, well marked, although a little overgrown in places, which contours the hillside then ascends steadily. Sparse forest cover gives way to open terraces, and 1hr 15mins from Sv Mihovil a small stone hut is reached. Continue up behind the hut and along a terrace to reach a junction in 5mins, where a trail on the left descends to the village of Žena glava. ▶ Turn right, initially along the top of a broad drystone wall, to reach

The route from Walk 23 joins Walk 22 here.

another junction in 15mins. Descend steeply to reach **Titova špilja** in a few minutes.

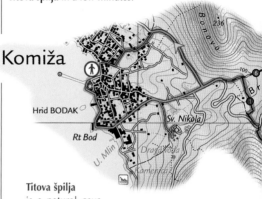

Komiža

Hrid BODAK

Rt Bod

Sv. Nikola

The church of Sv Duh, with Komiža visible in the bay below

Titova špilja
is a natural cave that was used as a secret base by Josip Broz Tito, leader of the Partisans and subsequently President of Yugoslavia, in 1944, when Croatia was under German occupation.

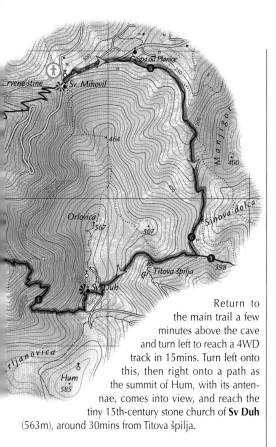

Return to the main trail a few minutes above the cave and turn left to reach a 4WD track in 15mins. Turn left onto this, then right onto a path as the summit of Hum, with its antennae, comes into view, and reach the tiny 15th-century stone church of **Sv Duh** (563m), around 30mins from Titova špilja.

From **Sv Duh** there are phenomenal views down over the Bay of Komiža and the headland projecting on the far side (Walk 24). The church was built in the 15th century, and according to a bishop writing in the 17th century processions would make their way up here. Note that the žig (stamp) on the wall beside the church has the height of Hum itself (587m).

▶ Walk down in front of the church a short distance (towards the summit of Hum), then turn right on

Do not try to climb to the top of Hum – this is a military area and access is prohibited.

a well-marked rocky trail which zigzags down the hillside towards Komiža. Go through several gates to reach the **main road** in 50mins. Turn left onto the road, then take a marked path on the right which leads to a 4WD track. ◀ Turn left onto this, then right on the main asphalt road. The first road on your right is the shortest route to the centre of **Komiža** and the bus stop (allow around 20mins, turning left off this down Podšpiljska, then left, then right).

Walkers making the ascent to Sv Mihovil from Komiža should follow this 4WD track then ascend Sv Mihovil via a steep path.

Variant route to Church of Sv Nikola

Keep straight ahead downhill and turn left to visit the prominent church of Sv Nikola, where a wooden fishing boat is burnt on St Nicholas' Day in honour of this patron saint of fishermen. Return to the road junction and turn left, then left again where the road forks, to soon arrive at the waterfront in Komiža. Follow this around to the right past the jetty and the tourist information office. The bus stop is just off the waterfront on the right on Ul Hrvatskih Mučenika, immediately after the post office.

WALK 23
Žena glava to Sv Duh (Hum) and Komiža

Start	Žena glava (245m)
Finish	Komiža (<5m)
Distance	7km
Time	2hrs 45mins
Terrain	Good rocky paths throughout; slightly steeper on descent to Komiža, with very short section of road walking at either end of route
Highest point	Sv Duh (563m)
Maps	Otok Vis Tourist and Trekking Map (HGSS, 1:20,000)
Access	Bus service along southern road between Vis and Komiža, via Podselje and Podšpilje (doesn't run every day). Get off at Podšpilje and walk uphill to village of Žena glava. Returning from Komiža at end of route is more straightforward (several buses run daily along 'newer' northern road).

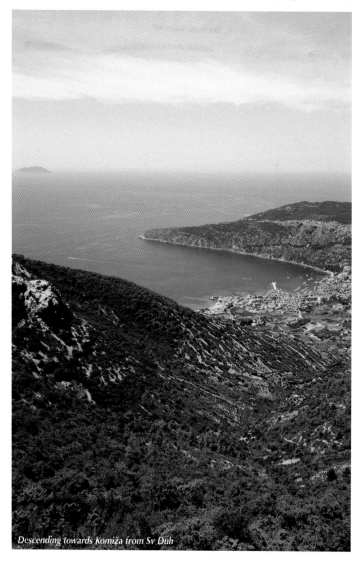

Descending towards Komiža from Sv Duh

A slightly shorter route to Sv Duh and Komiža than that described in Walk 22 starts from the village of Žena glava (the odd name means 'woman's head'). The route can be extended by starting at Vis town and walking along a 4WD road to Žena glava (see 'Other walks on Vis').

From **Žena glava** take the marked trail (the start of the trail is on the right after passing a large well, also on the right, just before the crest of the rise) and walk past houses. Then go steadily uphill, through wild rosemary, lavender and bay, with Hum and its antennae ahead. After 30mins the trail leads up onto a broad drystone wall (suhozid), which is followed to reach a junction with the trail from Gospa od Planice and Sv Mihovil (on Walk 22) in another 5mins. Keep straight ahead, following the route description for Walk 22. ◄ (Allow around 15mins from the junction to **Titova špilja**, a further 30mins to **Sv Duh**, and another 90mins for the descent to **Komiža**.)

See map on pages 181–180.

184

WALK 24
Komiža to Rt Barjaci, Dragodid and Sv Blaž

Start/Finish	Komiža (<5m)
Distance	7.5km
Time	2hrs 40mins
Terrain	Good rocky paths throughout, with very short section of road walking at either end of route
Highest point	280m (Rudine)
Maps	Otok Vis Tourist and Trekking Map (HGSS, 1:20,000). On the HGSS map Rt Barjaci is marked as 'Rt Barijoška'.
Access	Regular bus service between Vis and Komiža leaves from where ferry arrives in Vis and from Ul Hrvatskih Mučenika (by post office) in Komiža and travels the northern road between the two towns (another bus service follows southern road between them, but is much less frequent). Get off at last stop in Komiža.

A lovely walk along the headland to the north of Komiža Bay on good clear trails.

From the bus stop in **Komiža**, walk uphill and follow the road around to the left on Ulica Komiških iseljenika, past

Descending from Sv Blaž towards Komiža

185

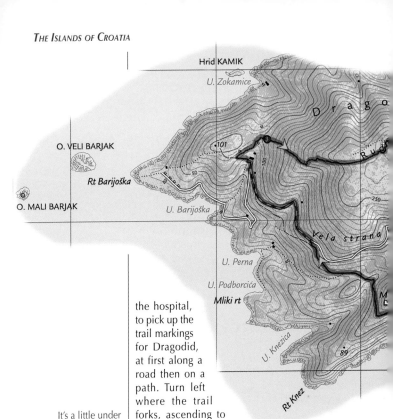

the hospital, to pick up the trail markings for Dragodid, at first along a road then on a path. Turn left where the trail forks, ascending to gain an excellent broad path, with good views of the island of Biševo. Take the second marked trail on the right, then turn left onto a 4WD track. Some 75mins from Komiža pass a 4WD track on the left which descends to the small, peaceful point at Rt Barjaci, likely to be deserted except for the occasional fisherman. ◄

It's a little under 30mins each way to go down the 4WD track to the small cove before Rt Barjaci – although the currents may be too strong for swimming.

Walk to the left of an old barracks building, following a fire-access track, then take a marked trail on the right. The rocky path ascends passing a ruined stone hut, then bears right along the top of a drystone wall (suhozid). Some 30mins from the deserted barracks pass a small area of walled polje (fields) with a well (marked

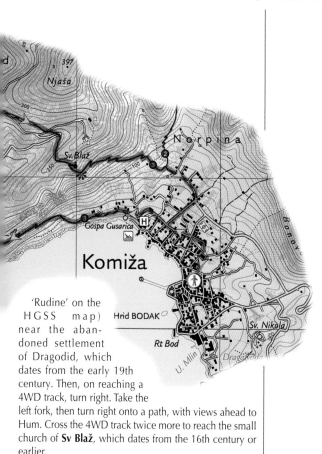

'Rudine' on the HGSS map) near the abandoned settlement of Dragodid, which dates from the early 19th century. Then, on reaching a 4WD track, turn right. Take the left fork, then turn right onto a path, with views ahead to Hum. Cross the 4WD track twice more to reach the small church of **Sv Blaž**, which dates from the 16th century or earlier.

Descend on a nice zigzagging cliff path to reach a junction 20mins from Sv Blaž. ▶ Turn right and descend to the houses, then continue straight ahead onto the asphalt road. Turn right onto Ulica Don Mihovila Pavlinovića, then left onto Ulica Komiških iseljenika, and veer right to reach the bus stop in the centre of **Komiža**, 35mins from Sv Blaž.

The trail on the left leads to the village of Oključna (around 75mins – route 2 on the recommended map).

OTHER WALKS ON VIS

Vis to Žena glava

It's easy enough to walk to Žena glava, at the start of Walk 23, from Vis town itself. An unsealed 4WD road branches left off the main road just outside Vis town near the supermarket (route 1 on the recommended HGSS map), or alternatively there is a path that ascends behind the old town (route 4 on the recommended HGSS map) over a saddle between the two hills of Veli vrh and Bratosavac; a 4WD road then leads through Cojno polje and joins up with the route from the supermarket, soon arriving at Žena glava.

Sv Andrija

A marked trail from behind Vis town (route 5 on the recommended map) leads up over the shoulder of Sv Andrija, the hill behind the town, passing the church of Sv Križ before joining a 4WD track which can be followed round to the right to the mountain hut (Pl kuća Sv Andrija, 270m; usually open at weekends during the summer, but check at the tourist information office or contact Željko Arnautović, tel. +385 (0)98 980 3330).

Vis to Stončica

This should be a great little walk from Vis town, but the paths, although once well marked, are now very overgrown in several places and poorly marked. Nevertheless there are plans to clear them again, and Stončica is a lovely bay, with a nice little beach (good for kids). It is possible to cycle there easily enough (currently the best way to get there) following the road from Vis town. The path from Stončica itself along the headland to the lighthouse at Rt Stončica is clear and easy to follow, with a good chance of seeing cormorants.

KORČULA

The walled medieval town of Korčula, with Sv. Ilija on the Pelješac peninsula in the background

South from Hvar, and separated by not much more than 1km from the tip of the Pelješac peninsula, Korčula is a lovely place which nevertheless sees far fewer visitors than Hvar or Brač. The two main towns, Vela Luka and Korčula town, are located at the west and east ends of the island respectively – the former at the head of a deep natural inlet; the latter on a small almond-shaped peninsula. Korčula town's stout walls, beautifully preserved historic core, and herringbone pattern of narrow streets and alleys make it one of the most attractive towns on the Adriatic (although it sees far fewer visitors than that other well-known walled medieval masterpiece

further south, Dubrovnik). The smaller towns of the island's interior, Blato and Smokvica, see very few visitors. The island becomes increasingly hilly towards its centre, with Klupca (569m), its highest point, lying between Pupnat and Smokvica – although the best for hiking is Kom (508m, Walk 27), rising between Blato and Smokvica. Some of the island's best beaches can be found around Lumbarda, southeast of Korčula town.

A local sword dance, the *moreška* – a distant relative of Morris dancing, but with blades clashing and sparks flying – is performed in Korčula town during the summer and is due to join the UNESCO List of Intangible

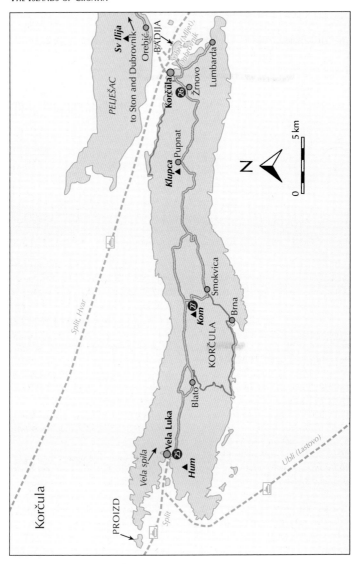

Korčula

PELJEŠAC

Sv Ilija
Orebić
to Ston and Dubrovnik
BADIJA
Otok Mljet/Dubrovnik
Korčula
26
Žrnovo
Lumbarda

Klupca
Pupnat

Split, Hvar

N
0   5 km

Smokvica
Kom 27
Brna

KORČULA

Blato

Vela spila
Vela Luka 25
Hum

Split

Ubli (Lastovo)

PROIZD

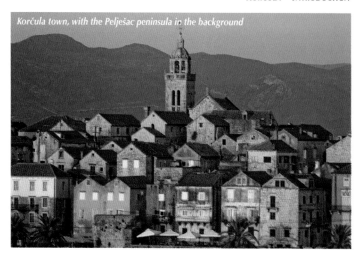

Korčula town, with the Pelj.šac peninsula in the background

Cultural Heritage in 2014. Another sword dance, the *kumpanija*, is performed less frequently in Blato, Vela Luka and elsewhere on the island.

Korčula town is frequently touted as the birthplace of the Venetian traveller Marco Polo – which it may, or may not, have been. However, Polo was possibly captured following an intense naval battle between the Venetians and the Genoese just offshore from here in 1298 (following which he wrote up his famous book of travels while lounging in a Genoese prison cell). The house in the old town where he is said to have lived is, in fact, later than his lifetime.

Two additional walks in the area are recommended (see 'Other walks on Korčula'; page 201). Vela spila, a large cave inhabited from the Paleolithic Era (some 18,000 years ago)

right through to at least the Bronze Age (about 2000BC), one of Croatia's most important archeological sites, is a pleasant 25min walk from the centre of Vela Luka (www.vela-spila.hr). The proximity of Korčula town to the Pelješac peninsula makes it a perfect base for a hike on Sv Ilija, the 961m peak which towers over the village of Orebić, directly opposite Korčula town on the peninsula.

Don't leave Korčula without trying Grk, the island's excellent white wine.

TOURIST INFORMATION

The tourist information office in Vela Luka is on the waterfront, about 10mins walk from the ferry/bus stop heading towards the town centre (Obala 3 br. 19; tel. +385 (0)20 813 619; www.tzvelaluka.hr). The tourist information office in Korčula town is on the west side of the old town walls by the waterfront (Obala dr. Franje Tuđmana 4; tel. +385 (0)20 715 701; www.visitkorcula.eu). The Blato Tourist Office is a 5min walk southeast of the bus station, by the park (Trg Dr. Franje Tuđmana 4; tel. +385 (20) 851 850; www.tzo-blato.hr). The Korčula Info website (www.korculainfo.com) also has plenty of useful information.

GETTING THERE AND GETTING AROUND

From Split there's a twice daily ferry service to Vela Luka, continuing to Ubli on the island of Lastovo. There's also a daily catamaran to Vela Luka, which calls at Hvar and continues to Lastovo, and a catamaran to Korčula town, which also calls at Hvar (all www.jadrolinija.hr). There's also a weekly ferry service between Rijeka and Dubrovnik (www.jadrolinija.hr) that calls at Split, Hvar and Korčula town. A car ferry runs from Orebić on the Pelješac peninsula to Dominče just outside Korčula town (www.jadrolinija.hr), and a small passenger boat plies the water between Korčula town itself and Orebić.

A regular local bus service runs between Vela Luka and Korčula town, via Blato, Smokvica and Žrnovo, which will drop walkers at the trailheads for Walks 26 and 27 (timetables available from the tourist information office or see www.autotrans.hr); another service runs between Korčula town and

Lumbarda. The Korčula–Vela Luka bus departs from the bus station in Korčula town and the point where the ferry and catamaran arrive in Vela Luka. Buses also run from Korčula town to Dubrovnik on the mainland, crossing on the Orebić–Dominče ferry and travelling via the Pelješac peninsula.

ACCOMMODATION

Private accommodation can be booked through the excellent Mediterano (www.mediterano.hr) in Vela Luka, or Kantun Tours (www.ikorcula.net) in Korčula town.

MAPS

Korčula Tourist and Trekking Map (HGSS, 1:25,000) – East (Istok) and West (Zapad) sheets are available from the tourist information offices in Vela Luka, Korčula and Blato. Walk 26 is on East sheet; Walk 25 is on West sheet; and Walk 27 is covered by both sheets. A less detailed Otok Korčula Tourist Map is available free from the tourist information office in Vela Luka.

OTHER ESSENTIALS

There are ATMs, pharmacies and supermarkets in Vela Luka, Korčula town and Blato. Vinum Bonum is an excellent little wine bar in Korčula town specialising in wines from Korčula and the Pelješac peninsula. Mediterano (www.mediterano.hr) in Vela Luka) offers bike rental.

WALK 25

Vela Luka to Hum

Start/Finish	Vela Luka bus stop (1m)
Distance	5.5km
Time	1hr 45mins
Terrain	Short section on asphalt, then a mixture of 4WD tracks and clear paths
Highest point	Hum (377m) (marked as 376m on recommended map)
Maps	Korčula Tourist and Trekking Map (HGSS, 1:25,000) – West (Zapad) sheet. Less detailed Otok Korčula Tourist Map, available free from the tourist information office in Vela Luka
Access	Regular bus service between Korčula town and Vela Luka. Bus stop in Vela Luka is by point where ferry departs.

A short, easy walk to Hum – a hill capped with the ramshackle ruins of an old fort – from Vela Luka, with surprisingly good views.

From the bus stop at the ferry departure point in **Vela Luka**, follow the main road (to Korčula town and Smokvica) uphill past the large factory building, then take the road on the right marked 'Hum'. Where the road splits into three, keep straight ahead, marked 'Pješačka staza' ('walking route'), then turn left onto a marked path after 5mins. Keep straight ahead onto a 4WD track, then turn left and downhill (still on a 4WD track), then go right and uphill on another 4WD track, with one brief shortcut on a path. Turn right onto a path, 35mins after leaving the main road, and soon zigzag up to reach the fort at the top of **Hum** (377m), 1hr from the main road.

The **fort**, known locally as *forteca*, was built by the Austro-Hungarians at the close of the 19th century on the site of an ancient hill fort. It was abandoned

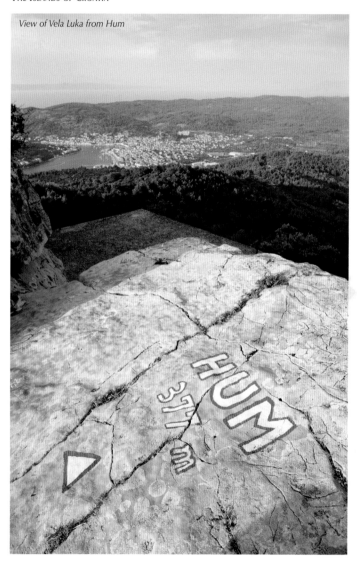

View of Vela Luka from Hum

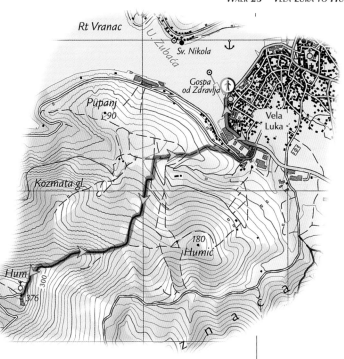

during the Italian occupation of the Second World War, and the interior was subsequently demolished. The views of Vela Luka are particularly good from here, and to the east, beyond the level fields of Blatsko polje, Kom (Walk 27) is clearly visible.

Descend to **Vela Luka** by the same route (allow 40mins).

WALK 26
Kočje

Start/Finish	Prvo selo (in Žrnovo) (155m)
Distance	4km
Time	1hr 40mins
Terrain	Some road walking (asphalt/4WD) at either end of route, with a rocky path in between
Highest point	215m
Maps	Korčula Tourist and Trekking Map (HGSS, 1:25,000) – East (Istok) sheet
Access	Regular bus service between Vela Luka and Korčula, leaving from where the ferry arrives in Vela Luka and from bus station in Korčula. Ask to be dropped at Žrnovo – more specifically Prvo selo (Žrnovo encompasses several hamlets) – look for café on left (if travelling from Korčula town). *If based in Korčula town*: option to walk to trailhead – from old town head west along coast road past Franciscan monastery, turning left uphill on minor road from the bay at Žrnovska banja.

A short, easy walk to an area of interesting karst scenery only a short distance from Korčula town. Kočje is a protected area, and visitors are asked by the tourist board to keep to established paths.

Turn right from the café in **Prvo selo** and follow the road northeast for 3mins, before turning left at a large cross on the road marked 'Brdo'. Follow the road uphill to the diminutive village of **Brdo**, continuing past the church to the far side of the village. Here pick up a 4WD track with faint trail markings and good views over the Pelješac channel. Ignore a path on the right (also with faint trail markings) before turning left onto a path (marked 'Kočje – Zaštićeni objekt prirode') to reach **Kočje**, around 25mins from Prvo selo.

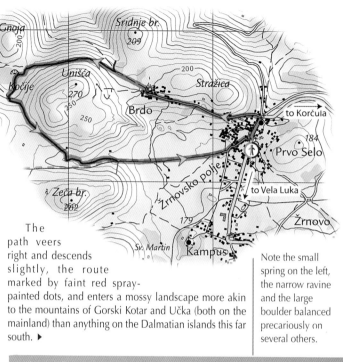

The path veers right and descends slightly, the route marked by faint red spray-painted dots, and enters a mossy landscape more akin to the mountains of Gorski Kotar and Učka (both on the mainland) than anything on the Dalmatian islands this far south. ▶

Note the small spring on the left, the narrow ravine and the large boulder balanced precariously on several others.

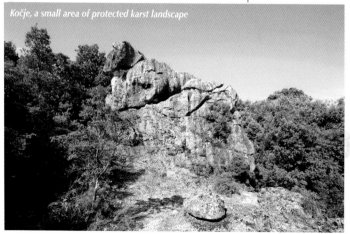

Kočje, a small area of protected karst landscape

Buses to Vela Luka stop by the war memorial, or cross to the opposite side of the road by the café for buses to Korčula town.

The path soon ascends slightly to a small clearing. Here continue straight ahead on a marked trail, following a path between drystone walls before gaining a rough 4WD track around 40mins after leaving the 4WD track on the other side of Kočje. Some 15mins later reach a shrine on the right. Turn left onto an asphalt road, and reach the war memorial opposite the café in **Prvo selo** in just under 5mins. ◀

WALK 27
Kom

Start/Finish	Mala Kapja (also written 'Kapja mala'), on the main road between Blato and Smokvica (145m)
Distance	4km
Time	2hrs
Terrain	Steady ascent on good, clear path, a large section of it through forest – so not too hot
Highest point	Kom (508m)
Maps	Korčula Tourist and Trekking Map (HGSS, 1:25,000) – East (Istok) or West (Zapad) sheet; **note** Mala Kapja is 'Kapja mala' on this map
Access	Regular bus service between Vela Luka and Korčula, leaving from where ferry arrives in Vela Luka and from bus station in Korčula. No official stop at Mala Kapja, so ask for 'Seosko domaćinstvo Mala Kapja' (a restaurant there) or say 'Za Kom'. The trailhead is on right side (if travelling from Vela Luka) of road just before bus turns right and goes downhill to Smokvica – look out for restaurant and prominent quarry at turnoff to Smokvica beyond.

A fantastic walk to one of the highest points on the island of Korčula, with outstanding views. Part of the clear, well-marked trail, passes through shady forest, then it follows a rocky path to the summit.

From the parking area by the main road at Mala Kapja, walk uphill on the asphalt driveway following the sign

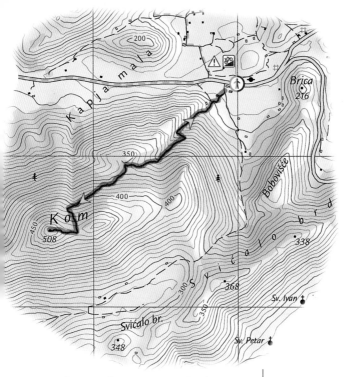

to Kom and passing the restaurant Seosko domaćinstvo Mala Kapja on the left. Take the right fork of this driveway by the farm building, then continue straight ahead up the clear path alongside a fence.

The trail ascends steadily, soon entering forest cover, and leads to a junction 30mins from the road. Turn left here (the trail is marked 'Jama') to arrive in 1min at the edge of Jama Komoračišće, an impressively large sink-hole which has been only partially explored. ▶

Return to the main trail and turn left (marked 'Kom'), passing a shady picnic area on the right in 5mins. After this the trail gradually becomes more open, pass-ing between large bushes of bay and Strawberry tree at around 400m before reaching the ridge. The trail leads over an open, bushy knoll, the air redolent with wild sage, and there are unbeatable views of Lastovo on the

Obviously you should not attempt to climb down into the sinkhole – the entrance is a 100m vertical drop.

left and the rocky summit cone ahead. From here it is less than 10mins to the top of **Kom** (508m).

Kom stands considerably higher than most of its surroundings, and the views, as might be expected from such an isolated summit, are outstanding. The island of Lastovo is prominent to the southeast, while Sv Nikola (the highest peak on the island of Hvar) and Sv Ilija (at the tip of the Pelješac peninsula) are clearly visible to the northwest and northeast respectively, and Vela Luka lies below to the west. The untended fields and overgrown olive terraces to the southeast and southwest are clear evidence of the move away from working the land over the past few decades. Expect to see plenty of butterflies around the summit, including Scarce swallowtail and Two-tailed pasha.

Return to Mala Kapja by the same route (allow 45mins). ◂

Remember that it's not an official bus stop in Mala Kapja, so make yourself clearly visible when flagging a bus down.

Vela spila

This large cave, inhabited from the Paleolithic Era right through to at least the Bronze Age, is an easy 25min walk from the centre of Vela Luka on a clearly marked concrete track (www.vela-spila.hr).

Sv Ilija (Pelješac)

Sv Ilija (961m), the highest point on the Pelješac peninsula and one of the best walks anywhere on the Croatian coast, can easily be climbed as a day trip if you're staying in Korčula town. Take the small passenger boat to Orebić from the waterfront beside the tourist information office in Korčula's old town, then walk from Orebić up past the Franciscan monastery and church. Then turn right and ascend on a clear path to the summit, which has outstanding views back along the spine of the Pelješac peninsula.

Sv Ilija, on the Pelješac peninsula, seen from Korčula town

LASTOVO

The small town of Lastovo

Of all the inhabited islands on the Croatian Adriatic, Lastovo is perhaps the least visited and the most unspoilt. Only around 10km long, it lies at the centre of a scattering of smaller islands, islets and reefs which make up Lastovo Islands Nature Park (Park prirode Lasovsko otočje). Together they constitute a remarkably rich and diverse concentration of wildlife and plants – including, on the crags of the Lastovnjaci and Vrhovnjaci islets, most of the Adriatic population of the endangered Audouin's gull. The island is quite mountainous, with its highest point, Hom (417m; Walk 28), near the centre of the island.

The Greeks founded a colony on the island in the fourth century BC (Ladesta, modern Lastovo town, which cascades down an inland-facing hillside in the northeast of the island), and there was a Christian basilica at Ubli, the island's other main settlement, as early as the sixth century AD. The island was a possession of the Republic of Dubrovnik from the 13th century until the arrival of Napoleon. Like its northwestern neighbour Vis, Lastovo was a military base when Croatia was part of Yugoslavia and was not open to foreign visitors until 1989. The oldest lighthouse on the Adriatic, built in 1839, stands sentinel on Struga, a headland at the southern tip of the island (see 'Other walks on Lastovo'; page 209). A distinctive feature of the houses on the island is the tall chimneys known as *fumari*.

At the end of Lent, Lastovo town holds its annual carnival, known as Poklad. Festivities culminate in an effigy being hauled across the town on a rope, paraded on a donkey and then burnt (not with the donkey, obviously). The symbolic humiliation and punishment of the luckless effigy is said to represent the unhappy fate of a messenger (called Poklad) sent by a fleet of Catalan pirates to demand the town's surrender – just before the fleet was destroyed by a miraculous storm. Anyone planning to visit the island around this time should book accommodation well in advance.

TOURIST INFORMATION

The tourist information office in Lastovo town is on the short main street (Pjevor bb; tel. +385 (0)20 801 018; www.tz-lastovo.hr). The Lastovo Islands Nature Park Office is in Ubli (Trg Svetog Petra 7; tel. +385 (0)20 801 252; www.pp-lastovo.hr).

GETTING THERE AND GETTING AROUND

Ubli can be reached from Split at least once a day by either ferry or catamaran (both www.jadrolinija. hr). The ferry calls at Vela Luka on Korčula, where passengers change onto another boat before continuing to Ubli; the catamaran calls at Hvar as well as Vela Luka. A local bus service runs between Ubli and Lastovo town, connecting with the ferry/catamaran departure and arrival times – timetables available from the tourist information office in Lastovo town. Buses depart from the waterfront where the ferry and catamaran arrive in Ubli, and from outside the church of Sv Roko at the end of the short main street in Lastovo town. The bus sometimes continues to Skrivena luka, depending on the number of passengers; otherwise a taxi will cost around

View of the island's southern coast and Struga peninsula, with the Struga lighthouse

80kn (contact Bartul Antičević, tel. +385 (0)95 517 2004). If you're staying at the campsite in Skrivena luka you could ask the owners to drop you at the church of Sv Marija just before Lastovo town, if they were driving there for supplies early in the morning (they usually do) – they won't ask for money but it would be reasonable to offer them some, since they have saved you a taxi fare.

ACCOMMODATION

There's only one hotel on the island, at Pasadur – which is not particularly recommended, and which in any case is inconveniently placed for the walk. Private accommodation is listed on the Lastovo Tourist Board website (www.tz-lastovo.hr). Camp Skriveni is a lovely quiet, remote, family-run campsite in the south of the island, with pitches in an olive grove (www.camp-skriveni.com, tel. +385 (0)91 196 3912).

MAPS

Park prirode Lastovsko otočje – Tourist and Trekking Map (HGSS, 1:20,000), available from the tourist information office in Lastovo town.

OTHER ESSENTIALS

There is an ATM, a small supermarket and a pharmacy in Lastovo town. Konoba Bačvara is a lovely family-run konoba towards the bottom of the old town (tel. +385 (0)20 801 131), and meals are also available at Camp Skriveni if you're staying there (including some of the best grilled fish you're likely to try anywhere, freshly caught and prepared by the owners).

WALK 28

Hom

Start/Finish	Church of Sv Marija u polju, on road to Skrivena luka below Lastovo town (25m)
Alternative finish	Camp Skriveni (50m)
Distance	11km
Time	4hrs 30mins; or 4hrs
Terrain	Some walking on asphalt/unsealed road, then a clear rocky path
Highest point	Hom (417m)
Maps	Park prirode Lastovsko otočje – Tourist and Trekking Map (HGSS, 1:20,000)
Access	Minibus between Lastovo and Ubli, connecting with ferry and catamaran arrival and departure times. Occasionally it also goes to Skrivena luka; otherwise taxis run from Lastovo town to Skrivena luka (see 'Getting there and getting around'). *From campsite in Skrivena luka*: possible lift or taxi to church of Sv Marija u polju (see 'Getting there and getting around'). *From Lastovo town*: follow one of flights of steps down through old town, bearing right to join main road to Skrivena luka near church of Sv Marija u polju.

A wonderfully remote-feeling route to Hom, the highest point on Lastovo, with a short section of road walking (very briefly on asphalt, then on 4WD tracks) followed by a good clear trail. There's a good chance of seeing Eleanor's falcon and other birdlife on the walk. An alternative route heads from the summit to finish at Camp Skriveni near Skrivena luka.

Sv Marija u polju ('Our Lady in the field'), the church at the beginning of the route, was built in the early 16th century on the foundations of an earlier 14th-century church. **Sv Ilija** (St Elias), on a low hill above the road, was built in the 16th century to invoke protection of the nearby fields from summer storms.

Walk south on the road from **Sv Marija u polju** until a marked path is reached on the right, which is followed up to the diminutive church of **Sv Ilija** in 15mins. Return to the road, turn right and then turn right onto a 4WD track signposted to Hom, Dubrova, Sv Luka and Zle polje. Follow the 4WD track between the fields and olive groves of Dubrova, taking a right fork and then keeping straight ahead past a 4WD track on the right, before turning left onto a marked path towards Hum. ◄

The 4WD track straight ahead leads to the little church of Sv Luka in 45mins (see 'Other walks on Lastovo'; page 209).

The path becomes a nice broad track over stone slabs, with views of Hom on the left. Keep straight ahead, passing unmarked paths to the left and right, then after passing through an area of pine forest turn left onto a 4WD track, then immediately right again on a marked path.

About 1hr after leaving the main Lastovo–Skrivena luka road reach **Veji pjevor**, a saddle, with Hom ahead. Beyond it and slightly to the right (west) are Veji greben and Pleševo brdo, capped with an antennae and a helicopter landing pad. Below on

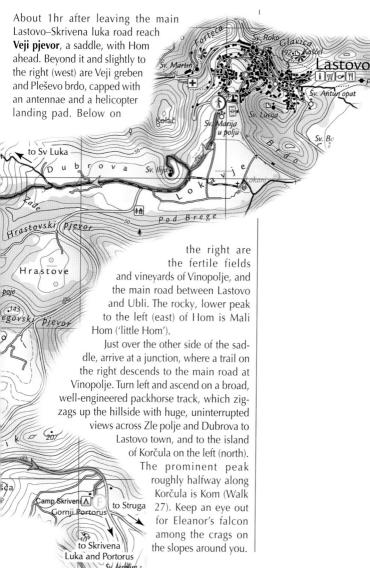

the right are the fertile fields and vineyards of Vinopolje, and the main road between Lastovo and Ubli. The rocky, lower peak to the left (east) of Hom is Mali Hom ('little Hom').

Just over the other side of the saddle, arrive at a junction, where a trail on the right descends to the main road at Vinopolje. Turn left and ascend on a broad, well-engineered packhorse track, which zigzags up the hillside with huge, uninterrupted views across Zle polje and Dubrova to Lastovo town, and to the island of Korčula on the left (north). The prominent peak roughly halfway along Korčula is Kom (Walk 27). Keep an eye out for Eleanor's falcon among the crags on the slopes around you.

View from the trail to Hom

About 40mins from the saddle the excellent, well-kept trail degenerates momentarily into a steep slope below a 4WD road and abandoned concrete barracks, from which walkers are separated by a low wire fence. Step over the fence onto the 4WD road and turn left (don't enter any of the buildings), then right uphill on a 4WD track which leads past antennae and generators to the ruined church of **Sv Juraj** on the summit of **Hom** (417m).

The church of **Sv Juraj**, now little more than a shell, dates from some time before the 15th century. There are good views northwest over some of the islands which make up the Lastovo archipelago – Prežba and Mrčara are two of the larger ones, which could be mistaken for part of the mainland from this angle, and also visible are the smaller Vlašnik and Bratin to the left (south) of these. Further afield is the island of Kopist, and beyond this Sušac.

Return to **Sv Marija u polju** and Lastovo town by the same route.

Alternative finish at Camp Skriveni

Alternatively, this route down from Hom provides a more
suitable option for those staying at Camp Skriveni (allow
1hr 15mins from summit of Hom), above Skrivena luka.
Turn right on the 4WD road below the summit, then left
where the road forks (signposted 'Portorus'). The 4WD
road sweeps around to the south of Veji greben and
Pleševo brdo in an extended loop, with lovely views
over untouched turquoise coves on the south coast of the
island and to the extended headland beyond Skrivena
luka, with Struga lighthouse (the oldest lighthouse on the
Croatian Adriatic, built in 1839) at its tip. About 55mins
from the summit of Hom reach the main road to Skrivena
luka and Portorus. Turn right onto this to reach the **campsite** in 20mins. ▶

It's a further 20mins
down to Skrivena
luka itself, and the
yachtie-dominated
cafés and beach on
the west shore of the
bay.

OTHER WALKS ON LASTOVO

Sozanj and Sv Luka

Sozanj, one of the better viewpoints on the island, is just
a few minutes' walk off the main Ubli–Lastovo road. Take
the minibus from Lastovo town towards Ubli, and ask
to be dropped off at the trail to Sozanj, which is on the
right (say 'Za Sozanj'). After hiking up to the viewpoint,
return to the main road and turn right for a short distance,
before turning left onto a path to the 11th-century church
of Sv Luka. From the church it is possible to follow a trail
left (west), joining a 4WD track to meet the route from
Lastovo to Hom at Dubrova in 45mins (see Walk 28).

Struga and Sv Čeberjan

Struga, the oldest lighthouse on the Croatian Adriatic,
was built in 1839. A 4WD road snakes its way around
the southeast shore of U Portorus beyond Skrivena luka
to Struga, passing a trail up to Čeberjan and the small
church of Sv Čeberjan (also written 'Sv Ciprijan') on the
way.

MLJET

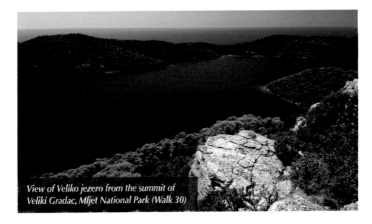

View of Veliko jezero from the summit of Veliki Gradac, Mljet National Park (Walk 30)

Mljet, which lies south of the Pelješac peninsula roughly halfway between Lastovo and Dubrovnik, is the most heavily forested island on the Adriatic, with tall stands of Aleppo pine, Holm oak and particularly dense maquis. The western part of the island, with its two saltwater 'lakes' (Malo jezero and Veliko jezero, Walk 29) connected to the sea by a narrow channel, was declared a national park in 1960. It supports an impressive concentration of wildlife, including the Indian grey mongoose, introduced in the early 20th century in an attempt to eradicate the island's sizeable population of snakes. The mongoose has thrived here ever since – at the expense of many other small native species as well as the snakes. There are several

moderate hills along the length of the island, the highest of them being Velji grad (514m; see 'Other walks on Mljet'; page 217) near the administrative capital of the island, Babino polje.

Legend tells that it was to Mljet that Odysseus was blown by the winds of Poseidon on his long journey home from the Trojan War; and some argue that it was on Mljet, not Malta, that St Paul was shipwrecked around AD60. The Illyrians were here around 2000BC – the remains of one of their hill forts can still be seen on the summit of Veliki Gradac (Walk 30). The island was settled by the Greeks (who called it Melita) in the fourth century BC and later by the Romans, who built a palace at Polače, the foundations of which survive. The island was given to

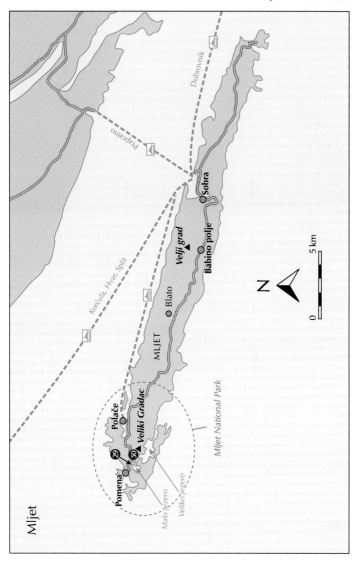

Mljet

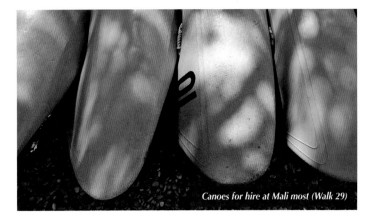

Canoes for hire at Mali most (Walk 29)

the Benedictines in the 12th century, when the monastery on the island of Sv Marija on Veliko jezero was built. From the 13th century until the arrival of Napoleon Mljet belonged to the Republic of Dubrovnik.

TOURIST INFORMATION

The Mljet tourist information office is in Babino Polje (Zabreće 2; www.mljet.hr), but also has offices in Sobra (tel. +385 (0)20 746 025) and Polače (tel. +385 (0)20 744 186).

GETTING THERE AND GETTING AROUND

There's a ferry from Prapratno on the Pelješac peninsula to Sobra (www.jadrolinija.hr), and a twice daily catamaran from Dubrovnik to Sobra, with one sailing continuing to Polače, and (in July–August only) to Korčula and Ubli (www.gv-line.hr). There's also a weekly ferry service between Rijeka and Sobra, calling at Split, Hvar and Korčula town before continuing to Dubrovnik (www.jadrolinija.hr).

ACCOMMODATION

Private accommodation is listed on the Mljet Tourist Board website (www.mljet.hr); the only hotel on the island is the Odisaj.

MAPS

National Park 'Mljet' Traveler's Map (1:14,000); available from National Park offices on Mljet

OTHER ESSENTIALS

There are a few shops and a pharmacy in Babino polje, and ATMs at Pomena and Polače.

WALK 29

Malo jezero

Start/Finish	Pomena (1m)
Distance	4km; or 6km
Time	1hr; or 1hr 45mins
Terrain	Easy lakeside path
Highest point	45m
Maps	National Park 'Mljet' Traveler's Map (1:14,000)

A short, easy walk in the most visited area of the national park, with an optional extension along the southwest shore of Veliko jezero.

After buying an entry ticket for the national park at the national park kiosk in **Pomena**, follow the road inland behind this, then take a path on the right marked 'Malo

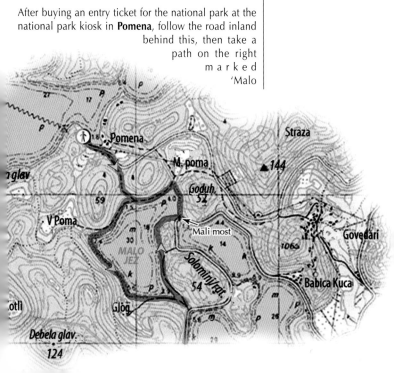

Turning left leads to Mali most, the bridge between Malo jezero and Veliko jezero, in about 10mins.

jezero'. This leads down through the trees to the shore of **Malo jezero** in 10mins. Here you have the option to walk in either direction around the lake. ◄ Follow the lake around to the right, marked 'kružni put' ('circular route').

> At **Mali most**, the small bridge dividing Malo jezero and Veliko jezero, is a national park kiosk, as well as a small beach and picnic area. It's also possible to hire bicycles and canoes here.

Soon reach a trail on the right, which is the start of an optional extension to the larger of the two lakes, Veliko jezero, and on to Sv Marija.

Extension to Veliko jezero
This route can be extended by about 1km (about 30mins) by continuing from Mali most along the southern shore of Veliko jezero to the bay behind the little island of **Sv Marija** with its monastery. Head on a short distance beyond this to Zakamenica, a viewpoint above the western shores of Mljet. Retrace your steps along the trail back to the lakeside, and turn right.

The trail continues around the lakeside, reaching Mali most in around 30mins. Continue around the northern shore of Malo jezero to return to **Pomena**.

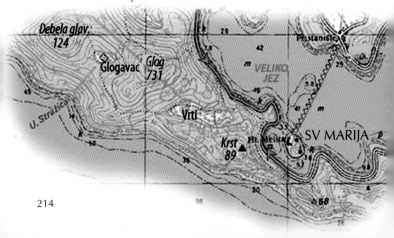

WALK 30
Veliki Gradac

Start/Finish	Pomena (1m)
Distance	6km
Time	3hrs
Terrain	Easy lakeside path followed by a section on asphalt, then a rocky path to the summit
Highest point	Veliki Gradac (157m)
Maps	National Park 'Mljet' Traveler's Map (1:14,000)

A slightly longer route than Walk 29, continuing to Veliki Gradac, with excellent views down over two lakes, Malo jezero and Veliko jezero.

Follow the route description (see Walk 29) from **Pomena** to Mali most, the small bridge spanning the channel between Malo jezero and Veliko jezero. From Mali most, follow the asphalt road along the northern shore of **Veliko jezero**, passing a few houses and cafés before heading away from the lake briefly to reach a junction.

There is an information office here, and the departure point for the **boat** out to the monastery on the island of Sv Marija is down to the right. The boat trip is included in the national park entry, although if you're visiting Mljet on a day trip, you might not have time to visit the monastery as well as Veliki Gradac.

Follow the road on the left up to the picnic area (marked 'ambulante'), then turn right onto a track passing the *groblje* (cemetery). Turn right onto the footpath marked 'Veliki Gradac', ascending with increasingly fine views and passing a trail marked 'polje' (fields) before reaching the modest summit of **Veliki Gradac** (157m, 90mins from Pomena), site of an Illyrian hill fort, from

where there are great views out over Veliko jezero.

Return to **Pomena** by the same route.

Veliki Gradac, once the site of an Iron Age hill fort

Velji grad

The highest point on Mljet, Velji grad (Veliki grad, 514m), is outside the national park boundary, and its summit is dominated by radio antennae. A route leads up from Babino polje to a saddle and then the summit in around 90mins, although a forest fire in the area has made some of the route hard to follow.

Mljet hiking trail

This 43km multi-day route between Pomena and Sobra was created in 2012 and covers more than half the length of the island. The route of the Mljet hiking trail (Mljetska planinarska obilaznica or MPO) goes from Pomena around the northwest coast then down to Goveđari; it heads across Veliki Gradac (160m, Walk 30), Montokuc (258m) and Veli Planjak (291m) to Blato; then goes via Špilja Ostaševica and Rogovići to Babino polje and Velji grad (514m), and finally on to Sobra.

APPENDIX A
Route summary table

Route	Title	Island	Distance	Time	Highest point	Page
1	Obzova	Krk	19.5km	5hrs 40mins	568m	63
2	Rt Škuljica	Krk	6km	2hrs	185m	69
3	Hlam	Krk	13km	3hrs 15mins	461m	72
4	Zakam and Jurandvor	Krk	5km	1hr 20mins	194m	77
5	Kamenjak	Rab	8km	2hrs 30mins	409m	85
6	Kamenjak to Matkići	Rab	5km	4hrs 40mins	409m	87
7	Premužićeva staza (Matkići to Lopar)	Rab	8km	2hrs 10mins	140m	91
8	Sis	Cres	2.5km	1hr 10mins	639m	99
9	Tramuntana	Cres	7km	3hrs 20mins	325m	101
10	Osorščica	Lošinj	12km	4hrs 45mins	588m	107
11	Veli Lošinj – The Dolphin Way	Lošinj	9.5km	3hrs 50mins	231m	112
12	Rt Vnetak	Unije	5.5km	1hr 15mins	<5m	121
13	Šimuni to Sv Vid	Pag	6.5km	2hrs 30min	348m	127
14	Dubrave to Sv Vid	Pag	2km	2hrs	348m	130
15	Šćah	Ugljan	4km	2hrs	288m	136

Route	Title	Island	Distance	Time	Highest point	Page
16	Oštravica, Orljak and Veli vrh	Dugi otok	6km	3hrs 10mins	328m	143
17	Kruševac	Dugi otok	3km	1hr	156m	147
18	Telašćica Bay and Mir jezero	Dugi otok	6.5km; or 23.5km	1hr 30mins; or 5hrs 10mins	50m; or 125m	149
19	Vidova gora	Brač	7.5km	3hrs 30mins	780m	157
20	Sv Nikola	Hvar	17.5km	5hrs	628m	165
21	Stari Grad Plain	Hvar	9km	2hrs	65m	170
22	Sv Mihovil to Sv Duh (Hum) and Komiža	Vis	7.5km	3hrs 15mins	563m	178
23	Žena glava to Sv Duh (Hum) and Komiža	Vis	7km	2hrs 45mins	563m	182
24	Komiža to Rt Barjaci, Dragodid and Sv Blaž	Vis	7.5km	2hrs 40mins	280m	185
25	Vela Luka to Hum	Korčula	5.5km	1hr 45mins	377m	193
26	Kočje	Korčula	4km	1hr 40mins	215m	196
27	Kom	Korčula	4km	2hrs	508m	198
28	Hom	Lastovo	11km	4hrs 30mins; or 4hrs	417m	205
29	Malo jezero	Mljet	4km; or 6km	1hr; or 1hr 45mins	45m	213
30	Veliki Gradac	Mljet	6km	3hrs	157m	214

APPENDIX B
Gateway cities – Rijeka, Zadar and Split

The following paragraphs contain travel essentials for the three main 'gateway cities' (the most convenient ferry departure points) for the islands covered by this guide.

Rijeka

Tourist information

Rijeka Tourist Board
(info centre at Korzo 14)
tel. +385 (0)51 335 882
www.tz-rijeka.hr

Transport

Ferries and catamarans leave from the long jetty near the town centre; the bus station is on Žabica, just west of the Korzo; the train station is a 10min walk west from this on Zvonimirova.

Recommended accommodation

Hotel Continental
www.jadran-hoteli.hr

Youth hostel
www.hfhs.hr

Recommended restaurants

Pizzerija Bracera (Kružina 12, an alley off the Korzo)

Ristorante Spagho (I Zajca 24)

Konoba Feral (Matije Gupca 5b)

Zadar

Tourist information

Zadar Tourist Board
Mihovila Klaića 1
tel. +385 (0)23 316 166
www.tzzadar.hr

Zadar County Tourist Board
Sv Leopolda B Mandia 1
tel. +385 (023) 315 316
www.zadar.hr

Transport

Most ferries and catamarans currently depart from Liburska obala, on the northeast side of the old town; the ferry for Lošinj departs from Gaženica, outside the town centre – a bus for Gaženica leaves from near the ferry ticket office, around 40mins before the ferry departure times. From 2014 the departure point for other ferry routes is planned to move to Gaženica as well (with a new bus route from the old town via the bus station), with only the Ugljan, Pašman and Dugi otok departures continuing from the old town – check at the tourist office or at the Jadrolinija ticket office on Liburska obala. Zadar's bus station is a 15min walk SE from the old town on Ulica Ante Starčevića. Zadar airport is at Zemunik, east from the city; a shuttle bus runs from Zadar bus station.

Recommended accommodation

Zadar Apartments
www.apartments-zadar-downtown.com

Hotel Bastion
www.hotel-bastion.hr

Hostel Forum
www.en.hostelforumzadar.com

Recommended restaurants

Pizzerija Tri Bunara (Trg tri bunari, behind Hotel Bastion)

Dva Ribara (Ulica Blaža Jurjeva 1)

Providenca (Varoška 6)

Some of the best ice cream in Croatia can be had from several ice cream shops along Kalelargo.

Split

Tourist information

Split Tourist Board
(info centre on the peristyle, Peristil bb)
tel. +385 (0)21 345

(info centre on the Riva, Obala HNP 9)
tel. +385 (0)21 360 066 606
www.visitsplit.com

Transport

Most ferries and catamarans depart from the ferry port by the bus and railway stations, on Obala Kneza Domogoja, under a 10min walk from Diocletian's Palace (some of the departure points, specifically those with a higher number, eg 'gat 23', are a 10min walk further along the waterfront from the main Jadrolinija office, so allow yourself enough time to get there), with a couple of catamaran services leaving from in front of the palace itself. Split airport is at Kaštela, about halfway between Split and Trogir – a shuttle bus leaves from the bus station in Split or you can take local bus 37 (from the local bus station on Domovinskog rata northeast of the palace, not the main one on the waterfront) towards Trogir, which goes past the airport but not into the airport car park.

Recommended accommodation
Villa Simoni
www.sobesimoni.com

Villa Matejuška
www.villamatejuska.hr

Goli & Bosi Design Hostel
www.gollybossy.com

Recommended restaurants
Kod Jože (Sredmanuška 4, beyond the park behind the palace)

Noštromo (Kraj Sv Marija 10, by the fish market)

Šperun (Šperun 3, in the Varoš neighbourhood)

APPENDIX C

Ferry routes

The following list gives a summary of the main ferry and catamaran routes relevant to this guidebook. Where a ferry/catamaran calls at a port on only some sailings (either at a certain time of day, or a certain day of the week) that port is listed in square brackets. Some of these routes are seasonal, operating a reduced service (or not calling at all ports) outside the summer months. For timetables and ferries to other islands, see the websites of different operators.

Key to operators		
J	Jadrolinija	www.jadrolinija.hr
GV	G&V Line	www.gv-line.hr
K	Krilo	www.krilo.hr
LNP	Linijska nacionalna plovidba	www.lnp.hr
RP	Rabska plovida	www.rapska-plovidba.hr

APPENDIX C – FERRY ROUTES

Key to type of boat

C	catamaran
F	ferry
FP	passenger only ferry

Ferry routes

Island	Route	Type	Operator
Lošinj	Zadar–[Silba]–[Ilovik]–Mali Lošinj–[Susak]–[Unije]–Pula	C	J
Unije	Mali Lošinj–[Srakane Vele]–[Unije]–Susak–Mali Lošinj	FP	J
Unije	Zadar–[Silba]–[Ilovik]–Mali Lošinj–[Susak]–[Unije]–Pula	C	J
Unije	Mali Lošinj–[Ilovik]–[Susak]–[Unije]–[Martinšćica]–Cres–Rijeka	C	K
Pag	Novalja–Rab–Rijeka	C	J
Pag	Žigljen–Prizna	F	J
Pag	Lun–Rab	FP	RP
Ugljan	Zadar–Preko	F	J
Pašman	Zadar–Tkon	F	J
Dugi otok	Zadar–Sali	FP	GV
Dugi otok	Zadar–Sali	C	GV
Dugi otok	Zadar–Brbinj	F	J
Brač	Split–Supetar	F	J
Brač	Split–Bol–Jelsa (Hvar)	F	J
Brač	Split–Milna–Hvar	C	J
Brač	Makarska–Sumartin	F	J
Hvar	Split–Stari Grad	F	J
Hvar	Split–Bol (Brač)–Jelsa	C	J
Hvar	Split–Milna (Brač)–Hvar	C	J
Hvar	Split–Hvar	C	K
Hvar	Split–Hvar–Korčula	C	J
Hvar	Drvenik–Sućuraj	F	J
Hvar	Rijeka–Split–Hvar–Korčula–Sobra (Mljet)–Dubrovnik	F	J

223

Ferry routes			
Island	Route	Type	Operator
Vis	Split–Vis	F	J
Vis	Split–[Hvar]–Vis	C	J
Korčula	Split–Vela Luka (Korčula)–Ubli (Lastovo)	F	J
Korčula	Split–Hvar–Vela Luka (Korčula)–Ubli (Lastovo)	C	J
Korčula	Split–Hvar–Korčula	C	J
Korčula	Rijeka–Split–Hvar–Korčula–Sobra (Mljet)–Dubrovnik	F	J
Korčula	Orebić–Dominče (Korčula)	F	J
Lastovo	Split–Vela Luka (Korčula)–Ubli (Lastovo)	F	J
Lastovo	Split–Hvar–Vela Luka (Korčula)–Ubli (Lastovo)	C	J
Mljet	Prapratno (Pelješac)–Sobra (Mljet)	F	J
Mljet	Dubrovnik–Šipan–Sobra–[Polače]–[Korčula–Ubli (Lastovo)]	C	GV
Mljet	Rijeka–Split–Hvar–Korčula–Sobra–Dubrovnik	F	J

APPENDIX D
Further reading

Guidebooks
Rudolf Abraham, *Walking in Croatia* (2nd edn; Cicerone, 2010)

Rudolf Abraham, *National Geographic Traveler Croatia* (2nd edn; National Geographic, 2014)

Rudolf Abraham and Thammy Evans, *Istria. The Bradt Travel Guide* (Bradt, 2013)
– the most detailed guide to the Istrian peninsula

Piers Letcher, *Croatia. The Bradt Travel Guide* (5th edn; Bradt, 2013)

History
Catherine Wendy Bracewell, *The Uskoks of Senj. Piracy, Banditry, and Holy War in the Sixteenth-Century Adriatic* (Cornell University Press, 2011)
– an excellent in-depth study of the Adriatic's most famous pirates

Aleksander Durman (ed), *One Hundred Croatian Archeological Sites* (Leksikografski zavod Miroslav Krleža, 2007)

Florin Curta, *Southeastern Europe in the Middle Ages 500–1250* (Cambridge, 2006)

Misha Glenny, *The Fall of Yugoslavia* (London, 1992)
  – a good account of the war in the former Yugoslavia

Ivo Goldstein, *Croatia: A History* (London, 1999)

Dimitri Obolenski, *The Byzantine Commonwealth: Eastern Europe, 500–1453* (London, 1971)

Laura Silber and Allan Little, *The Death of Yugoslavia* (London, 1995)
  – an account of the war in the former Yugoslavia based on the excellent BBC TV series

Marcus Tanner, *Croatia: A Nation Forged in War* (Yale, 1997)

John Wilkes, *The Illyrians* (Oxford, 1992)

Natural history

E Nicolas Arnold and Denys W Ovenden, *Reptiles and Amphibians of Europe* (Princeton Field Guides, 2002), reprinted from the second edition of *Collins Field Guide to the Reptiles and Amphibians of Britain and Europe* (Harper Collins, 2002)

Klaas-Douwe B Dijkstra and Richard Lewington, *Field Guide to the Dragonflies of Britain and Europe* (British Wildlife Publishing, 2006)

Gerard Gorman, *Birding in Eastern Europe* (Wildsounds, 2006)
  – covers the best birding sites in Croatia and several other countries in Eastern Europe

Gerard Gorman, *Central and Eastern European Wildlife* (Bradt, 2008)

Sanja Kovačić et al, *Flora Jadranske obale i otoka* (Školska kniga, Zagreb, 2008)
  – a useful local field guide, in Croatian, which includes the 250 most common species of flowering plants on the Croatian coast and islands

Oleg Polunin, *The Concise Flowers of Europe* (Oxford, 1972)

Oleg Polunin, *Flowers of Greece and the Balkans: A Field Guide* (Oxford, 1987)

Lars Svensson, Peter J Grant, Killian Mullarney and Dan Zetterström, *Collins Bird Guide* (2nd edn; Harper Collins, 2010), also published as *Birds of Europe* (2nd edn; Princeton University Press, 2010)
  – an outstanding field guide to European birdlife

Tom Tolman and Richard Lewington, *Collins Butterfly Guide* (Collins, 2009)

Language

Celia Hawkesworth with Ivana Jović, *Colloquial Croatian: The Complete Course for Beginners* (Routledge, 2007)

David Norris, *Complete Croatian: Teach Yourself* (Teach Yourself, 2010)

APPENDIX E
Croatian language notes and glossary

Pronunciation
Pronunciation is very important if you are to be understood clearly. As a number of Croatian letters are not found in the English alphabet, and some familiar letters are pronounced differently in Croatian (in particular j, which sounds like an English 'y'), a list of letters requiring particular attention is given below.

a – pronounced as the 'a' in father
c – pronounced as the 'ts' in cats
č – pronounced as the 'ch' in church
ć – very similar to č, but slightly softer, as the 'tj' sound in picture
đ – pronounced as the 'j' in jam
dž – very similar to the above
e – pronounced as the 'e' in egg
g – pronounced hard, as the 'g' in give
i – pronounced as the 'i' in ill
j – pronounced as the 'y' in yes
lj – pronounced as the 'lli' in million
nj – pronounced as the 'ni' in onion
o – pronounced as the 'o' in hot
r – rolled slightly
š – pronounced as the 'sh' in shake
u – pronounced as the 'oo' in pool
ž – pronounced as the 's' in pleasure, or the French 'j' in janvier

Other letters are pronounced as they would be in English.

The complete Croatian alphabet is as follows:

a, b, c, č, ć, d, đ, dž, e, f, g, h, i, j, k, l, lj, m, n, nj, o, p, r, s, š, t, u, v, z, ž.

Note that there is no q, w, x or y.

Glossary
The following list reflects variations in vocabulary/dialect most likely to be encountered on the coast/islands. Where this differs significantly with 'standard Croatian' as spoken in Zagreb, the 'standard' version is listed in square brackets. Alternative masculine/feminine/plural endings are given, where appropriate, as are some variations in meaning.

Greetings, introductions and basic phrases

Hello/Good day	Dobar dan
Hi/bye! (informal)	Bog/Adio!
Good morning	Dobro jutro
Good evening	Dobra večer
Good night	Laku noć
Goodbye	Do viđenja
Have a good trip!/	
Safe journey!	Sretan put!
Yes	Da
No	Ne
Please	Molim
Thank you	Hvala
Thank you very much	Puno hvala/ hvala vam lijepo
I beg your pardon?	Molim?
Sorry!	Oprostite!/Pardon!
Excuse me (when about to request something)	Oprostite
Excuse me (when trying to get past someone)	Samo malo
Just a minute!	Samo malo!
Here you are! (when offering something)	Izvolite!
Cheers! (as a toast)	Živjeli!
Do you speak English/French?	Govorite li engleski/ francuski?
I'm sorry, I don't speak Croatian	Oprostite, ne znam hrvatski
I don't understand	Ne razumijem
I don't know	Ne znam
How are you? (formal)	Kako ste?
Fine, thank you	Dobro, hvala
Pleased to meet you!	Drago mi je!
Where are you from?	Odakle ste?
I'm English	Ja sam Englez
I'm from… (England/Scotland/Ireland)	Ja sam iz… (Engleske/Škotske/Irske)
I'm a… (teacher/ student/engineer…)	Ja sam… (profesor/student/inženjer…)
Mr	Gospodin
Mrs	Gospođa
I like/I don't like…	Sviđa mi se/ne sviđa mi se…
Great!	Odlično!
Please could I have…	Molim vas…
Do you have…?	Imate li…?
How much does it cost?	Koliko košta?
Can I order, please?	Mogu li naručiti?
I've already ordered, thank you	Već sam naručio, hvala
Can I pay, please?	Mogu li platiti?
Can I have the bill, please?	Molim vas račun?
One ticket to…, please	Jednu kartu do…, molim
What time does the ferry/catamaran to … leave?	U koliko sati ide trajekt/ katamaran za …?
Which platform/ dock?	Koji peron/gat?
There is/there are… /is there?/are there…?	Ima…/ima…?

General vocabulary

after	poslije
and	i
before	prije
big	veliki
closed	zatvoreno

227

cold	hladno	4	četiri
difficult/more difficult	teško/teže	5	pet
easy/easier	lako/lakše	6	šest
excellent	odlično	7	sedam
far	daleko	8	osam
fast	brzo	9	devet
from	iz	10	deset
from... to...	od... do...	11	jedanaest
here	ovdje/tu	12	dvanaest
hot	vruće	13	trinaest
how?	kako?	20	dvadeset
in	u	21	dvadeset jedan
later	kasnije	30	trideset
much/many	puno/mnogo	40	četrdeset
near	blizu	50	pedeset
now	sada	60	šezdeset
of	od	70	sedamdeset
on	na	80	osamdeset
open	otvoreno	90	devedeset
or	ili	100	sto
slow	polako	1000	tisuća
small	mali		
that	ono/to		

Time, days of the week and months

there	tamo
this	ovo

What time is it?	Koliko je sati?
09.25	devet i dvadeset pet sati
14.00	dva sata/četrnaest sati

to	u (sometimes na is used instead)
under	ispod
very	jako/vrlo
what?	što?/ča?
when?	kad?
where?	gdje?
who?	tko?
with	s/sa
without	bez

minute	minuta
hour	sat
day	dan
week	tjedan
month	mjesec
year	godina
Sunday	nedjelja
Monday	ponedjeljak
Tuesday	utorak
Wednesday	srijeda
Thursday	četvrtak
Friday	petak
Saturday	subota
January	siječanj

Numerals

0	nula
1	jedan
2	dva
3	tri

February	veljača
March	ožujak
April	travanj
May	svibanj
June	lipanj
July	srpanj
August	kolovoz
September	rujan
October	listopad
November	studeni
December	prosinac
today	danas
tomorrow	sutra
yesterday	jučer
in the morning	ujutro
in the afternoon	popodne/poslije podne
in the evening	navečer

Transport

aeroplane	avion
airport	zračna luka/aerodrom
arrivals/departures	dolazak/odlazak
boat	brod
bus	bus
bus station	autobusni kolodvor
bus stop	stajalište
by train	vlakom
car	auto
catamaran	katamaran
dock	gat
ferry	trajekt
on foot	pješice
platform	peron
taxi	taksi
ticket	karta
ticket office	blagajna
single ticket	u jednom smjeru
return ticket	povratna karta
train	vlak
train station	željeznički kolodvor

Directions and rights of way

north	sjever
south	jug
east	istok
west	zapad
up	gore
down	dole
(on the) left	(na) lijevo
(on the) right	(na) desno
Where are you going? (formal)	Kamo idete?
I'm/we're going to…	Idem/idemo u…
Excuse me, where's the path to…?	Oprostite, gdje je put za…?
How far is…?	Koliko daleko je…?
Is it marked?	Je li markiran?
I'm/we're lost!	Izgubio sam se/izgubili smo se!
path	staza
road	cesta
unsealed road	bijela cesta/makadam
way	put

Warnings, danger and emergencies

Danger!	Opasnost!
Be careful!	Pazi!
Help!	U pomoć!
doctor	doktor/liječnik
ambulance	hitna pomoć
Please call a doctor!	Molim vas pozovite doktora!
I fell/he fell/she fell	Pao sam/pao je/pala je
sick/ill	bolestan
hospital	bolnica
snakebite	zmijski ugriz
blood	krv

broken	slomljen
landmines	mine
abandoned	
military installation	napušteni vojni objekt

Landscape features

cave	špilja/spila/pećina
cliff	stijena
crag, bare limestone peak	kuk
drystone wall	suhozid
drystone wall enclosures for sorting sheep	mrgari
type of ancient drystone shelter	trim
field/level area between limestone ridges	polje
footpath	pješačka staza
forest	šuma
hill	brdo
lake	jezero
limestone/karst	kras
limestone depression	vrtača/doline
limestone pit	škrapa
mountain	planina
mountain hut	planinarski dom/ planinarska kuća
mountain range	planinski lanac
pass	vrata/prijevoj/sedlo
path	staza
peak/summit	vrh
pond	lokva/lokvica
ridge	greben
river	rijeka
rock/rocky	kamen/kamenit
scree	sipar
shelter	sklonište
sinkhole	jama
small peak, hillock	glava (literally 'head')
spring	izvor
steep	strm
valley	dolina
water	voda
stamp	žig

On the coast

bay	uvala
beach	plaža
cape/headland/point	rt
coast	obala
island	otok
peninsula	poluotok
sandy	pješčan
sea	more
stony/pebbly	šljunčan

Weather

It's raining	Pada kiša
Will it rain today/ tomorrow?	Hoće li padati kiša danas/sutra?
It's getting dark	Pada mrak
It's windy	Puše vjetar
The bura is blowing	Puše bura
weather	vrijeme
cloud	oblak
fog	magla
hail	tuča
ice	led
lightning	munja
rain	kiša
snow	snijeg
storm	oluja
sun	sunce
thunder	grom
wind	vjetar
wind (NE)	bura

Hiking equipment

book	knjiga
boots	čizme
gloves	rukavice

hat	kapa
jacket	jakna
(mountain) map	(planinarska) karta
mountain	
guidebook	planinarski vodič
rucksack	ruksak
sleeping bag	vreća za spavanje
sleeping mat	karimat
socks	čarape
tent	šator

Accommodation

apartment	apartman
bathroom	kupaonica
bed	krevet
campsite	kamp
hostel	hostel
hotel	hotel
key	ključ
room	soba
single room	jednokrevetna soba
double room	dvokrevetna soba
reservation	rezervacija
half board	polupansion

Towns and cities

ATM	bankomat
bank	banka
bookshop	knjižara
bridge	most
castle	kaštel/dvorac
cathedral	katedrala
chapel	kapelica
chemist	apoteka/ljekarna
church	crkva
citadel/old town	stari grad
door	vrata
entrance	ulaz
exit	izlaz
exchange office	mjenjačnica
garden	vrt

graveyard	groblje
house	kuća/dom
market	pijaca/tržnica
monastery	samostan
post office	pošta
restaurant	restoran/konoba /gostionica
shop	dućan/trgovina
square	trg
street	ulica
town/city	grad
tower	kula
village	selo
wall	zid
waterfront	riva

Plants and animals

animal	životinja
bat	šišmiš
beech	bukva
bird	ptica
butterfly	leptir
swallowtail	lastavičji rep
buzzard	škanjac
cat	mačka
cow	krava
cypress	čempres
deer (roe)	jelen
deer (red)	srna
dog	pas
donkey	magarac
duck	patka
eagle	orao
falcon	sokol
peregrine falcon	sivi sokol
fish	riba
flower	cvijet
fox	lisica
goat	koza/jarac
griffon vulture	bjeloglavi sup
holly oak	crnika

horse	konj
juniper	borovica/smrika
lizard	gušter
mosquito	komarac
mouflon	muflon
mountain pine	klekovina/planinski bor/bor krivulj
mouse	miš
oak	hrast
olive tree	maslina
pine	bor
rabbit	zec
rosemary	ružmarin
sage	kadulja
sheep	ovca
snake	zmija
common viper	šarka/šarulja
nose-horned viper	poskok
spider	pauk
squirrel	vjeverica
swallow	lastavica
thyme	majčina dušica
tree	drvo/stablo
wild pig	divlja svinja

Food and drink

Fruit (voće)

apple	jabuka
orange	naranča
fig	smokva
grapes	grožđe
pear	kruška
plum	šljiva
strawberry	jagoda
walnut	orah
water melon	lubenica

Fish (riba) and other seafood (plodova mora)

shellfish	školjke
lobster	jastog
oysters	kamenice
mussels	dagnje
octopus	hobotnica
squid	lignje
tuna	tuna

Meat (mesa)

beef	govedina
chicken	piletina
ham	šunka
lamb	janjetina
sausages	kobasice
veal	teletina

Vegetables (povrće)

aubergine	patliđan
beans	grah
cabbage	kupus
carrot	mrkva
courgette	tikvice
cucumber	krastavac
garlic	češnjak
lettuce	zelena salata
mushroom	gljiva
onion	luk
potato	krumpir
salad	salata
spinach	špinat
tomato	pomidor/paradajz [rajčica]

Drinks (piće)

beer	pivo
coffee	kava
coffee (espresso)	espresso/obična kava
coffee with milk	kava s mlijekom
fruit juice	voćni sok
apple juice	sok od jabuke
orange juice	sok od naranče
milk	mlijeko
red wine	crno vino

tea	čaj	*eggs*	jaje
water	voda	*food*	jelo
mineral water		*fried/deep fried*	prženo/pohano
(sparkling/still)	mineralna voda	*grilled*	na žaru
	(gazirano/negazirano)	*homemade*	domaće
tap water	obična voda	*ice cream*	sladoled
white wine	bijelo vino	*lunch*	ručak
		main course	glavno jelo
Other		*olive oil*	maslinovo ulje
bread	kruh	*pasta*	tjestenina
brown/		*pizza*	pizza
white bread	integralni/bijeli kruh	*pepper*	papar
breakfast	doručak	*rice*	riža
cake	kolač	*salt*	sol
cheese	sir	*sauce*	umak/saft
chocolate	čokolada	*soup*	juha
dessert	desert	*sugar*	šećer
dinner	večera		

APPENDIX F
Contacts and useful addresses

Embassies and cultural centres in Croatia

British Embassy in Zagreb
Ivana Lučića 4
PO Box 454
10000, Zagreb
Tel: +385 (0)1 600 9100

British Consulate in Dubrovnik
Vukovarska 22/1
Mercante centar
20000 Dubrovnik
Tel: +385 (0)20 324 597

British Consulate in Split
Obala Hrvatskog narodnog
preporoda 10/III
21000 Split
Tel: +385 (0)21 346 007

Croatian National Tourist Board
UK Office (London)
Tel: 020 8563 7979

Croatia (Head Office, Zagreb)
Tel: +385 (0)1 469 9333
www.croatia.hr

Regional tourist boards
Kvarner County Tourist Office
www.kvarner.hr

Split Dalmatia County Tourist Board
www.dalmatia.hr

Zadar County Tourist Board
www.zadar.hr

Dubrovnik and Neretva County Tourist Board
www.visitdubrovnik.hr

For local tourist boards, see the introduction to each island.

Bus and train times
Autotrans
www.autotrans.hr
A good place to start for bus times; one of Croatia's largest transport networks, covering many of the islands

Bus times
www.autobusni-kolodvor.com
This shouldn't be taken as a definitive list of bus times; searching through the relevant tourist information office, bus company or bus station will usually show more results

Zagreb bus station (with timetables)
www.akz.hr

Train times
www.hznet.hr
Click on 'HŽ Putnički prijevoz', then select language, then click on 'timetables'

Driving
HAK (Croatian Automobile Club)
www.hak.hr

Croatian Motorways
www.hac.hr

Cycling
www.pedala.hr
www.bicikl.hr/bike-bed
www.mojbicikl.hr

Croatian government departments

State Institute for the Protection of Nature
www.dzzp.hr

Croatian Meteorological Service
www.meteo.hr

Hydrographic Institute of the Republic of Croatia
www.hhi.hr

Croatian Bureau of Statistics
www.dzs.hr

Ministry of Foreign Affairs
www.mvp.hr

State Geodetic Administration (Državna geodetska uprava)
www.dgu.hr

Wildlife and conservation

Snakes of Croatia
www.zh.zadweb.biz.hr

Croatia Birding
www.croatiabirding.com

Matt's European Butterflies
www.eurobutterflies.com

Lepidapp
www.lepidapp.co.uk

European Butterflies and Moths
www.lepidoptera.pl

Moths and Butterflies of Europe and North Africa
www.leps.it

Blue World Institute of Marine Research and Conservation
www.blue-world.org

Accommodation

Croatian Camping Union
www.camping.hr

Croatian Youth Hostel Association
www.hfhs.hr

Apartmanija
www.apartmanija.hr

Lighthouses of Croatia
www.lighthouses-croatia.com

Gdje na more?
www.gdjenamore.com

Mountaineering and mountain rescue

Croatian Mountain Rescue Service (Hrvatska Gorska služba spašavanja, HGSS or GSS)
www.gss.hr

Croatian Mountaineering Association (Hrvatski planinarski savez)
www.hps.hr

Other useful websites

ACI Club
www.aci-club.hrInformation on sailing, including marinas

Croatian Diving Association
www.diving-hrs.hr

SMAND (hiking maps)
www.smand.hr

Visit Croatia
www.visit-croatia.co.uk

LISTING OF CICERONE GUIDES

Tour of the Queyras
Tour of the Vanoise
Trekking in the Vosges and Jura
Vanoise Ski Touring
Via Ferratas of the French Alps
Walking in Corsica
Walking in the Auvergne
Walking in the Cathar Region
Walking in the Cevennes
Walking in the Dordogne
Walking in the Haute Savoie – North & South
Walking in the Languedoc
Walking in the Tarentaise and Beaufortain Alps

GERMANY

Germany's Romantic Road
Hiking and Biking in the Black Forest
Walking in the Bavarian Alps
Walking the River Rhine Trail

HIMALAYA

Annapurna
Bhutan
Everest
Garhwal and Kumaon
Langtang with Gosainkund and Helambu
Manaslu
The Mount Kailash Trek
Trekking in Ladakh
Trekking in the Himalaya

ICELAND & GREENLAND

Trekking in Greenland
Walking and Trekking in Iceland

IRELAND

Irish Coastal Walks
The Irish Coast to Coast Walk
The Mountains of Ireland

ITALY

Gran Paradiso
Sibillini National Park
Stelvio National Park
Shorter Walks in the Dolomites
Through the Italian Alps
Trekking in the Apennines
Trekking in the Dolomites
Via Ferratas of the Italian Dolomites: Vols 1 & 2
Walking in Abruzzo
Walking in Sardinia
Walking in Sicily
Walking in the Central Italian Alps
Walking in the Dolomites
Walking in Tuscany
Walking in Umbria
Walking on the Amalfi Coast
Walking the Italian Lakes

MEDITERRANEAN

Jordan – Walks, Treks, Caves, Climbs and Canyons
The Ala Dag
The High Mountains of Crete
The Mountains of Greece
Treks and Climbs in Wadi Rum
Walking in Malta
Western Crete

NORTH AMERICA

British Columbia
The Grand Canyon
The John Muir Trail
The Pacific Crest Trail

SOUTH AMERICA

Aconcagua and the Southern Andes
Hiking and Biking Peru's Inca Trails
Torres del Paine

SCANDINAVIA

Walking in Norway

SLOVENIA, CROATIA AND MONTENEGRO

The Islands of Croatia
The Julian Alps of Slovenia
The Mountains of Montenegro
Trekking in Slovenia
Walking in Slovenia: The Karavanke

SPAIN AND PORTUGAL

Costa Blanca: West
Mountain Walking in Southern Catalunya
The Mountains of Central Spain
The Northern Caminos
Trekking through Mallorca
Walking in Madeira
Walking in Mallorca
Walking in Menorca
Walking in the Algarve
Walking in the Cordillera Cantabrica
Walking in the Sierra Nevada
Walking on Gran Canaria
Walking on La Gomera and El Hierro
Walking on La Palma
Walking on Tenerife
Walking the GR7 in Andalucia
Walks and Climbs in the Picos de Europa

SWITZERLAND

Alpine Pass Route
Central Switzerland
The Bernese Alps
The Swiss Alps
Tour of the Jungfrau Region
Walking in the Valais
Walking in Ticino
Walks in the Engadine

TECHNIQUES

Geocaching in the UK
Indoor Climbing
Lightweight Camping
Map and Compass
Mountain Weather
Moveable Feasts
Outdoor Photography
Polar Exploration
Rock Climbing
Sport Climbing
The Book of the Bivvy
The Hillwalker's Guide to Mountaineering
The Hillwalker's Manual

MINI GUIDES

Alpine Flowers
Avalanche!
Navigating with a GPS
Navigation
Pocket First Aid and Wilderness Medicine
Snow

MOUNTAIN LITERATURE

8000m
A Walk in the Clouds
Unjustifiable Risk?

For full information on all our guides, books and eBooks, visit our website: **www.cicerone.co.uk**.

Walking – Trekking – Mountaineering – Climbing – Cycling

Over 40 years, Cicerone have built up an outstanding collection of 300 guides, inspiring all sorts of amazing adventures.

Every guide comes from extensive exploration and research by our expert authors, all with a passion for their subjects. They are frequently praised, endorsed and used by clubs, instructors and outdoor organisations.

All our titles can now be bought as **e-books** and many as iPad and Kindle files and we will continue to make all our guides available for these and many other devices.

Our website shows any **new information** we've received since a book was published. Please do let us know if you find anything has changed, so that we can pass on the latest details. On our **website** you'll also find some great ideas and lots of information, including sample chapters, contents lists, reviews, articles and a photo gallery.

It's easy to keep in touch with what's going on at Cicerone, by getting our monthly **free e-newsletter**, which is full of offers, competitions, up-to-date information and topical articles. You can subscribe on our home page and also follow us on **Facebook** and **Twitter**, as well as our **blog**.

Cicerone – the very best guides for exploring the world.

CICERONE

2 Police Square Milnthorpe Cumbria LA7 7PY
Tel: 015395 62069 info@cicerone.co.uk
www.cicerone.co.uk